YEHUDI MENUHIN MUSIC GUIDES

Violin and Viola

YEHUDI MENUHIN MUSIC GUIDES

Available
Piano by Louis Kentner

In preparation
contributions on
Bassoon by William Waterhouse
Clarinet by Jack Brymer
Double bass by John Gray
Flute by James Galway
Guitar and lute by Narcisco Yepes
Harp by Sidonie Goossens
Horn by Barry Tuckwell
Oboe by Leon Goossens and Edwin Roxburgh
Percussion by James Holland
Trumpet by Sidney Ellison

To follow
contributions on
'Cello
Conducting and orchestration
Harpsichord and early keyboard instruments
Organ
Trombone and tuba
Voice

Yehudi Menuhin with two of the children from his school

YEHUDI MENUHIN MUSIC GUIDES

Violin and Viola

*Yehudi Menuhin
and William Primrose*

with a section on the
history of the instrument by
Denis Stevens

MACDONALD AND JANE'S · LONDON

First published in Great Britain in 1976 by
Macdonald and Jane's,
Macdonald and Company (Publishers) Limited,
Paulton House,
8 Shepherdess Walk,
London N.1.

ISBN Cased: 0 356 04715 6
       Limp: 0 356 04716 4

Typesetting by Bedford Typesetters Limited

Made and printed in Great Britain by
Hazell Watson & Viney Ltd,
Aylesbury, Bucks

Contents

vi

List of Illustrations

ACKNOWLEDGEMENTS

Editorial Board:

General editor: Yehudi Menuhin

Coordinating editor: Patrick Jenkins

Advisers: Martin Cooper
                          Eric Fenby
                          Robert Layton
                          Denis Stevens

Drawings: Ian Fleming and Associates;
                          Nancy Hidden

Music examples: Malcolm Lipkin

Jacket: David Farrell

The Hindemith sonata in chapter 10 is reprinted by courtesy of Schott and Co.

The purpose of this series is not to impose a new set of musical disciplines, nor to attempt to provide a blue-print for yet another teaching 'method'; but to stimulate in the musical young (as well as students of all ages) a still finer, and better informed, response to the instruments of their choice and to the world of music they contain.   P.J.

By its very existence, this book is a tribute to my darling Diana, whose love, wisdom and goodness, whose extraordinary fusion of authority with selflessness, and whose pervading beauty, are the qualities which enable her fortunate companion to transform his dreams into realities – or in any case to transform our constant faint echoes of eternity into palpable living sound, however ephemeral, in humility and pride.

Y.M.

Yehudi Menuhin's Preface

The violin, delicate and small as it is, holds too much of the history of man, his creative gifts, his craftsmanship, his emotion and thought, to be encompassed by any one writer. A performer brings the violin to life and makes it sing, and this may be the ultimate function of the violin as the bridge between the one and the many. But he does not necessarily know all about its history, its constituent parts and the supremely skilled workmanship that goes into the making of a great instrument. I am, therefore, all the more happy and grateful to those who have fulfilled the inherent scope of the subject. To Denis Stevens for his sense of patient scholarship and for his insight into the origins and development of the instrument we know as the violin today. To Etienne Vatelot, that most eminent craftsman, who has spoken so pertinently about the composition of the violin. And very particularly to Bill Primrose; even though I have ventured into the viola literature and adore playing the instrument, I could not presume to write about it with the authority of a man who has given it his whole life, nor could I have written with the wit and originality that mark his chapter.

The Instrument
by Etienne Vatelot

The violin is made up of 82 or 84 pieces of wood, over and above which the belly or the back is made up of one or two pieces.

The woods used are maple for the back, the ribs and the scroll, pine for the belly, ebony for the fingerboard, and boxwood, rosewood or ebony for the pegs, tail-piece and tail-pin.

The success of the instrument's resonance depends on several factors: on the choice and age of the wood, on the design of the contours, on the curve of the table and of the back, on the thicknesses, on the tension of the bass-bar supporting the belly, on the fluidity of the varnish, on the adjustment of the tension and the position of the sound-post (a small cylinder of deal wedged between the belly and the back) which needs only to be a tenth of a millimetre out of place to alter the sound, on the cut of the bridge, on the angle made by the strings and their place on the bridge, and on the diameter of the strings.

To all these factors are added the taste and even the character of the violinist, who looks to his instrument not only for power and resonance but also for a reflection of his own personality.

The violin maker therefore must not only pay attention to the physical condition of the violin, which varies according to climate, and consequently hygrometry, but also keep the instrument in a state of receptivity for the actual violinist who will have the responsibility and the talent to play it.

As for the bow, made from a Brazilian wood, it must be both strong and supple, both light and balanced. The horsehair

3

The Instrument

is attached at one end to the head and at the other to the frog of the bow. It is held by a tail-pin attached by a screw hook. The strands of this horsehair must be both strong and elastic and usually come from Canada or Siberia.

Depending on the quality of the bowstick, the bowmaker can decorate the frog with such precious materials as ivory, tortoiseshell and gold. But however beautiful a bow may appear, only the violinist can judge its worth.

Part One

The Violin
by Yehudi Menuhin

One
The Violin and the Violinist

A platonic relationship – the violinist and his violin

In observing the violin and the bow – for the two are inseparable – I am led to wonder whether this twin pair bear any relationship to the bow and arrow, their murderous forebears. Is the archer's bow the precursor of the violin, having acquired a resonance chamber? Is the violin bow the arrow, as it crosses the strings and sends the sound to its heartfelt destination? Did the twanging gut tensed between the bow ends evolve into the taut violin string, or alternatively into the violinist's bow, which in turn is taut with horsehair until stick and hair become resilient? Be that as it may, the violin perhaps represents the most astonishing evolution and sublimation of that murderous weapon – one of the few tools of man not designed to kill, one of the most perfect embodied and yet disembodied forms directed to the contact of spirit and soul rather than to physical impact.

Its shape is in fact inspired by and symbolic of the most beautiful human object, the woman's body. There are no straight lines in the violin; every line is curved and bent, embracing and delicate. We speak of its parts anatomically: head, neck, shoulders, waist, belly, back – and bottom. The varnish on a Stradivarius or a Guarnerius evokes the sun caught in the silken texture of human skin. And like the female human voice, the violin combines the entire soprano and contralto range. I have often wondered whether psychologically there is a basic difference between the woman's relationship to the violin and the man's. I have always kissed the head of my violin before putting it back to sleep,

7

as it were, in its case. I have always gazed at the iridescent, living and altering reflection of the beautiful varnish as I shift the violin in its angle to the light; and I have always looked upon that translucence and fire as the temperament of a human being. Does the woman violinist consider the violin more as her own voice than the voice of one she loves? Is there an element of narcissism in the woman's relation to

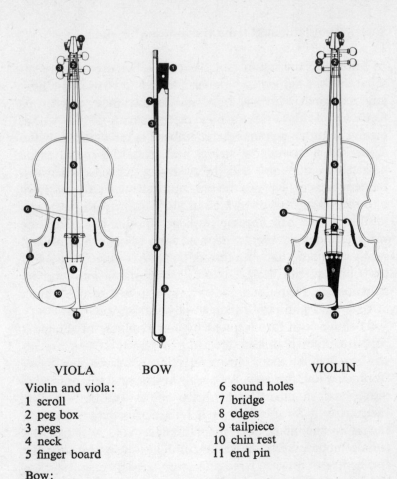

VIOLA   BOW   VIOLIN

Violin and viola:
1 scroll
2 peg box
3 pegs
4 neck
5 finger board

6 sound holes
7 bridge
8 edges
9 tailpiece
10 chin rest
11 end pin

Bow:
1 frog
2 leatherpiece
3 winding

4 bow stick
5 hair
6 tip or point

The Violin and the Violinist

the violin, and is she, in fact, in a curious way, better matched for the cello? The handling and playing of a violin is a process of caress and evocation, of drawing out a sound which awaits the hands of the master. It is enticing and fascinating, passive if you wish, but ready to respond at the slightest touch. A beautiful violin contains that infinite potential – of sound, flexibility, colour, intonation, pitch and volume – which awaits the music and the musician.

Paradoxically, however, tactile contact with the violin is strictly limited. There is the delicate contact between the chin and the chin-rest; between the collar-bone and the lower violin edge; and between the thumb and a finger of the left hand and the neck (except when the hand rises to the higher positions well above the neck). But otherwise contact is restricted to the working surface of the finger-board, and it is on this that the violinist spends his lifetime of concentration. There are no visible mileposts and, blindly but surely, he must discover in this field of action, limited in space, the infinite scope which mastery reveals. Accuracy of placement of fingers, accuracy of touch and vibration, accuracy of each motion, vertical or horizontal or sideways, rolling or oscillating – these are the means with which he can express the whole gamut of human emotion and evoke the response of his audience wherever they may be and however they are constituted.

With his right hand he must develop an equally sensitive feel for the stick, for its weight and resistance, for the quality of the sound which each type of motion achieves – whether the bow is floating or exerting its weight or pressure, whether his hold is loose or gripping, and whether the bow, within its narrow range, moves farther or closer to bridge or finger-board. From the velvet-covered sound of the finger-board to the squeaking, whistling ponticello quality nearer the bridge, the bow must draw the sound through the strings, crossing them at right angles. This right angle is one of the very few nearly perfect right angles in the violin, just as the arrow crosses what might be considered the shape of half a violin when it shoots out at right angles to the line of the taut gut.

9

Part One: The Violin

When it is at rest (when that gut is not pulled back), the bow – drawn over the strings, high above the violin, in fact at its highest point where the strings reach the bridge – is drawn directly above what are known as the F holes. Let no irreverent thought cross the reader's mind! It is from these lovely, graceful, elongated openings that the sound emerges.

Then there is the contact between the chin-rest and the chin – the chief anatomical distinction between man and ape. Anatomically, any ape or monkey could play a piano or a cello, blow a flute, or thump a drum, but because of the chin requirement only the *homo sapiens* can play a violin.

In olden days, before the higher positions of the fingerboard were explored, when the violinist did not have to find that perfect, balanced and delicate hold which enables him to travel at lightning speed from one end of the fingerboard to the other, the chin-rest was not required. In fact the violin was often held almost at the waist. It gradually rose until it reached the neck. Then the chin was often placed on the right side of the tail-piece, and on most old violins the varnish shows signs of wear and erosion on the lower right hand corner of the top of the violin, as well as on the left, proving that the method of holding it between chin and shoulder – or, as it should be, between chin and collar-bone – was not yet defined very precisely and was left more or less to the personal inclination and constitutional shape of the bones of each player. Even today chin-rests come in the most varied and often quite ludicrous shapes and sizes, some very high, some low, some tilted, some cup-shaped, some ridged, some meticulously small, some like giant saucers; but they all place the chin either to the left of the tail-piece or directly above. I believe the chin should touch – touch, mind you, not press on – the violin in the centre, just to the left, very nearly above the tail-piece, because the violin should be free to roll between the thumb and fingers, on both sides of an imaginary line through its centre.

Also, it must always be remembered that this living entity which is the violin, when being played, must nowhere be squeezed or pressed upon, but left free to vibrate. Thus the

10

shoulder should never lay a wide surface against the bottom of the violin. Rather must the violin touch the collar-bone and transmit its vibrations through the bone to the amplifying resonating spaces of the body itself, whilst the shoulder is left free to move flexibly back and forth and even sideways – part of the mechanical gear of the violinist and so essential in contributing to the freedom of the muscles of the shoulder and the neck. These vibrations are not limited to the violin but are also transmitted to the bow and to the fingers of the right hand holding the bow. It is, in fact, important to practise holding the bow so delicately that you gradually acquire the sensation of the vibrating horsehair and stick. It is only by developing such subtleties of sensation that you can master the art of violin playing.

Otherwise and everywhere the violin should not be touched or handled except when cleaning and polishing – and some-times, as a great treat, always with clean hands, stroked only once, and only once in a while, with the back of the fingers to feel the texture of its beautiful varnish.

Thus the violinist's relationship with his instrument must remain physically platonic, confined to the finest work and workmanship, and for ever sublimated in beautiful sound which is given to all to hear.

Space and sensation – the violinist and his body

We must remember, in considering the violin, that it is also a child of space. The bow and arrow is a dense affair and controls but a single shaft. The violin, on the other hand, is a resonating hollow and spreads its sound in a wide area. It is the carrying quality of the sound as well as the space, inside both the violin and the player, which makes this whole world of vibrations one which demands and controls the empty spaces – the interstices between matter, the spaces between men – and joins them in common experience and in common bond.

The sound is coaxed and drawn out of a violin. The action is a pulling of the string, which sets the string, and the violin, and the air, and the player, in vibration. It is not a pressing of the string downwards; it is not a crushing of the violin. Perhaps the sublimation of weapon into musical instrument is precisely this special element which brings a wider area, both within and without, into sympathetic vibration.

To achieve this the player must control and include as much space as possible within his motions. His body should be as delicately balanced and poised, as fluid in its motions, as the continuity of sound which is characteristic of the violin. There should be no break, no interruption: from the toes to the head there should be an impulse travelling without obstacle. Vertical space (that is height, from which the limbs are allowed to fall by degree, which means that their weight is released by degree) and horizontal embrace (that is an embrace which does not constrict, but rather widens the circle, as when the two hands, the two sets of five fingers, touch) combine to create the widest possible space, within a circle which, for example, spreads the shoulder blades to increase the space between them. The physical implications of these requirements will be considered in later chapters.

I personally believe that the player should also be purged of narrow, confining thoughts and emotions, for it is only by stretching and emptying that space is created. Breadth, clarity and openness – almost vacuums – must be cultivated in the mind as well as the body. Within and without, the violinist and his instrument should strive to control the maximum amount of space.

This is, in fact, a territorial imperative. For the violinist, like the bird, sings so that he may be heard over the widest area. The most wonderful violin is the one with the widest carrying capacity. Even a pianissimo can be heard in the farthest reaches of the Royal Albert Hall; seven or eight thousand people can sit spellbound, and concentrate on this wisp of beautiful sound reaching their hearts.

But this power to dominate the realms of space comes from the triumph of sublety and degree. The strength of a violinist's performance, his attack and incisiveness, are derived in

12

the first place from the delicacy of his sensation. If he can develop an awareness of the millionth of a grain rather than of an ounce, of an ounce rather than of a pound, he is on his way to becoming a violinist. Otherwise he tends to brutalize his instrument, the composer's music and himself. The penalties are the frustrations and the physical and mental deformities of so many violinists, who have knocked their heads against a wall, who have demanded instead of entreated. Demand there must be, but demand contained in patience, faith and perseverance, and not in headlong and sudden attack.

Two

The Preparation of the Violinist

Physical preparation

It is vital to appreciate that playing the violin always makes a severe demand on the body's stamina and balance. It cannot be forced; it can be exerted and tired, but it should never be tensed.*

Exercises. I think it is important to have a series of exercises which always begin from the least strained position, that is of course lying on your back on the floor, the body stretched and breathing easily.

In this position lift and stretch one foot, say the left, and lift and stretch backwards one arm, say the right. The stretch must extend to the tips of your fingers and to the tips of your toes or the bottom of your heels. At the same time lift your head and turn it in the direction of the stretched arm. Then alternate this with the opposite limbs. This strengthens the stomach muscles, and you can simply and at any time relax into an impassive state of lying on your back.

Then develop this exercise into a circular motion. Raise both legs and both arms and your head, and swing the arms round. This necessitates raising your body on to either the right hip or, in the opposite swing, the left hip. As your body moves on to the right hip, twist your trunk in the opposite direction anti-clockwise, and *vice versa*. This also strengthens the stomach muscles and encourages circulation. As soon as

---

*I appreciate that many musicians, whom I admire, do not agree with my regime; but the books in this series are designed to represent the personal opinions of the authors.

you have had enough, just let everything fall to the ground, and continue to lie back quietly.

You can do the same exercise on your stomach. Lifting your head, stretch your left arm with your right leg and turn your head towards your left arm. Then alternate with your right arm and left leg.

You can also lift both arms and both legs simultaneously and, in a kind of breast stroke, swim, with nothing touching the ground except your stomach. This straightens the muscles of the back, so important in standing; also the muscles of the bottom.

When lying on your stomach, put your chin on the ground and raise your head by opening and closing your jaw. Then, with your head on one side and with the weight on your jawbone, move your jaw laterally, again raising your head. These are excellent exercises for violinists, as we must develop the muscles of the jaw and the chin.

Another good exercise, a prelude to lying on the ground, is to fall on your knees with your bottom touching your heels. Lean forward until your head touches the ground, then spread your shoulders, and stretch your arms straight ahead. In this position, with the lungs full of air, try to force the air into your back and expand your lungs still further. This stretches the vertebrae.

Another experiment is, while lying on your back, lifting your head with one hand on the back of your head. Allow your head to give its full weight to the hand supporting it, say the left one. Then with your right hand on the chin, turn your head, which must be quite loose and relaxed on your neck, in a clockwise direction as it would be seen by someone looking from behind at the crown of your head. The left hand on the back of your head throws it to the left and the right hand on the chin pushes it to the right. You will notice that, if the neck is not quite relaxed, it will crack in the joints of the vertebrae. This is a good thing; it should never be strained, but it is excellent to release the tension in the neck. Then do it the other way round: the right hand and palm hold the back of your head while the left one is on your chin.

Another extremely fine exercise, also to do with the relaxation of the neck and the looseness in it, is to pull your head directly back, with the interlocked fingers of both hands supporting it from underneath and with the thumbs encircling and bracing your neck, so that your thumbs show at the front of your neck. Stretch your neck, with the aid of your arms working against your shoulders. Pull your head in a straight line, following the line of the vertebrae, until you lie straight back on the floor, flat.

These last two exercises should always be done after standing on your head to release whatever constriction may occur in your neck from the weight of your body on your neck.

Of course, in the perfect headstand the neck is so strengthened that it actually stretches, and the body is stretched from the head to the tips of the toes so that it is elongated, not only in the neck but also along the whole length of the vertebrae.

Stretching and twisting your limbs is extremely important, for they can only relax when they have been stretched to their full length, which is somewhat more than most people think it is. The twisting releases whatever impediments and catches there may be in your joints and bones.

Relaxation. The violinist must also learn the apportionment of time. He must learn to practise efficiently. He must know when he must rest, when to play, when to sleep, when to read. He must try to establish a relationship between his private and his public life. He must assess the value, excitement and stimulus of travel, the importance of holidays.

As far as relaxation is concerned, inverting the position of the body, to compensate for the standing and the swinging of violin playing, is an excellent way of resting. Try a Yoga headstand or shoulder-stand, perhaps against a wall; or lie down with your legs over a chair; or – as I often do – lie upside down in an armchair with your knees over the top and your head on the floor; or lie with your back over a footstool and both feet and hands touching the ground. Whenever the violinist gets tired, or his arms feel limp or

16

strained, he should, I believe, immediately take up one of these positions. Alternatively, lie on the ground, breathe and stretch; then lie quietly and passively until a new wave of warmth and potential flows through your veins and you are ready to resume.

If you are under heavy strains – nervous, spiritual or emotional – I personally believe that you will be helped by Yoga deep breathing and the immobile balancing poses of the different *asanas*.

These postures are particularly beneficial in relieving the burden on your heart and blood circulation – for remember that the violinist's hands, when playing, are always on the level of the heart if not above. Another useful aid is to fill two basins – one with hot, one with cold water – and dip the forearms, including the elbows, into first one and then the other alternately about three or four times, longer in the hot water than in the cold. Then lean your head against something cool, and rest stretched out on the floor or on a bed for some twenty minutes.

It is a good thing for the violinist to practise some sport, such as ping pong or tennis; weight-lifting is excellent, or you can use the bar to hang your body from the hands, knees or feet. It is important, however, always to perform compensating exercises. If you lift weights you must also stretch the body. If you do fast motions you must also exercise by means of the slowest possible movements.

Diet. I have always believed in a healthy diet. No white sugars, but instead honey, date sugar or cane juice; lots of fruit; a minimum of animal fats, but instead sesame or sunflower oil; much less meat than is usually consumed. As for alcohol, that, in my opinion, should be taken as a special treat. My advice is not to drink much when playing regularly. And, of course, tobacco should be eschewed, for it inhibits the lungs and the whole respiratory system. Drugs, tranquillizers, aspirin and everything which might create little clots of blood throughout the system should be avoided.

17

Part One: The Violin
How body exercises work

One of the difficulties in teaching any movement, especially a very subtle one, is that it is almost impossible to communicate the sensation which must precede the movement. The student is, therefore, always trying to imitate a visual image and this, in fact, is a great drawback, for in following his active will he is suppressing the consciousness of the subtle without which the visible movement itself cannot happen.

I have evolved the following series of exercises inspired by a booklet on Tai Chi, a Chinese form of exercise. This consists of the delicate adjustments in the body to a shifting centre of gravity. It is readily understood that when lying on the ground on your back, arms on the floor at your sides, your centre of gravity is along your spine. By raising your right arm, the support which the weight of the right arm gave your body is lost and your body rolls slightly, very slightly (it is a diagonal roll), towards the right. This actually happens before the arm leaves the ground, when you begin to carry the weight from your shoulder. This applies whether you raise an arm or a leg. The corresponding concomitant rolling and tilting in the rest of the body always accompanies the lifting of any limb. Legs must be lifted from the hip.

As you lift a given limb, each section should be felt to hang from the upper part. Lift an arm, for example. Separately test the weight of each part as it hangs from the upper arm (elbow, forearm, wrist) until, finally, each finger, and the thumb, is felt to fall separately and independently. The arm can be rotated: either allow the hand to fall from the wrist laterally, or, by rotating further clockwise, allow the wrist to drop backwards. The same exercise should be done with legs, concentrating on ankles and knees.

While raising an arm or a leg, breathe in, and time the motion so that by the time you reach the apex of the motion (that is at right angles to the floor pointing to the ceiling) your lungs are filled. Lower the limb relaxedly, and with a slow exhalation. The exhalation can take the form of a hum on

18

whatever note generates the greatest vibration throughout .your body.

The leg exercises should be repeated on each side, raising the leg sideways up in the air from the hip. In fact, the hip moves laterally, raising the leg before any visible leg movement occurs. Do the same exercise lying on your stomach, with your head resting sometimes on one cheek, sometimes on the other. These exercises are particularly good not only for strengthening, but also for relaxing, the shoulders; and for gaining an extraordinary degree of control and relaxation in the limbs and the body.

One of the great qualities of exercises such as these is that they bridge that moment between zero effort and 0.0001 effort. What I am trying to say is that so many of our movements begin with a jerk, or a deliberate effort of will, ignoring the very gradual preparatory changes which precede the visual movement. It is these first, pre-visual adjustments which hold the key to subtle, precise and easy movements. Stiffness resides in the loss of smooth *initial* movement, even *before* any visual evidence occurs, *not*, as commonly and mistakenly believed, merely in the shrinking of amplitude.

It can be observed that a lifting movement of any given limb originates in the furthest, biggest joint. Our joints begin at both extremities with the smallest (fingers, toes) and as we travel (in our mind) to the centre of the body, we come to the biggest (hips, shoulder blades). In between these two pairs of large floating anchors is our flexible, adaptable spine. The *initial* sensation of a limb movement is a preparatory muscle movement at hips or shoulder blades, undetectable by the eye, but palpable to the touch, and an accommodating rearrangement – rolling, tilting – of the spine and body to readjust the centre of gravity. Every rolling or tilting motion is (1) a passive adjustment to gravity and (2) a diagonal one.

Breathing, also, should be as smooth as your body motions. You will notice that by expanding your ribs laterally before inhaling, the inhalation occurs very smoothly and without any initial jerk.

Part One: The Violin
Breathing exercises

Let us begin with space and breath without the violin.

Lie flat on the floor (on a mat or rug), your arms extended without effort alongside your body. Then lift one arm slowly to the vertical position whilst inhaling. The speed at which the arm is raised should be dictated by the length of inhalation. At the vertical position, stretch upwards. Feel the weight of the arm and the weight of each individual part of it (fingers, wrist, forearm) as you relax; stretch again; and then allow the arm to fall slowly to its original position, the speed determined by length of exhalation.

Begin each movement (still in the horizontal position) by extending your shoulder. In the movement of raising an arm, motive power is located in the shoulder, while arm, wrist and fingers are relaxed. Learn to feel the decreasing weight of the limb as the vertical is reached, and its increasing weight as the limb moves towards the horizontal. Exhalation can be accompanied by a hum between barely touching lips.

Do the same with your legs, one at a time, ankles and knees relaxed, power coming from the hip. Stretch in the vertical position, and time your movements with inhalation and exhalation. Repeat the leg exercise with your arms behind your head, beginning in the extended position on the floor. Do the same raising and lowering your head.

Repeat the first exercise, beginning in one extended position (arms by sides) and ending in the other (arms above head on floor), making a full half circle. Now do this with both arms together, moving in parallel and also in opposite directions. Repeat the pattern with both legs together. Then the left arm and the right leg together. In fact, try any combination which occurs to you.

Lying on your right side, do the same exercise raising the leg and arm alternately, then repeat this on the left side. Lying on your stomach, arms extended alongside your body, repeat these exercises, but you will naturally find the range of movement smaller.

Now stand up. Raise an arm (from a limp, hanging position)

to horizontal, to vertical, to stretched, all on inhalation; then lower it to a hanging position on exhalation. Now do this with the other arm. Then with both arms. Then describe as near full circles as possible. Begin the circle first with your arms rising in *front* of your body and falling (slowly with exhalation) behind your head, and then practise the opposite circle with arms rising well *behind* your body and falling in front of it. Learn to feel the changing distribution of weight and its effect on your body balance.

With hands interlocked and arms stretched above your head, bend your body forwards whilst rolling back on your heels, and backwards whilst rolling forward on your toes.

Lift one leg, then one leg and an arm, always slowly to inhalation and exhalation. Learn to feel the continual changes in the balancing requirements of your body.

Mental and spiritual preparation

To maintain himself in the best physical condition, the athlete knows the importance of exercise, sleep and proper diet. But I believe that the violinist, in addition, has a further obligation. He knows that he cannot play and interpret unless his spiritual condition is as good as his physical. The state of mind, the state of nerve, the state of heart are as important as the state of muscle.

An athlete is dominated by the will to win, but for a violinist the competitive spirit is not nearly enough, for he must communicate something more than the capacity to amaze and stimulate, something more even than perfect discipline and perfect form.

Just as grains of sand take on orderly symmetrical patterns when laid on a flat vibrating surface, so, it seems to me, do the vibrations of music coordinate and reorder into harmonious symmetrical patterns all the elements of a human being's thoughts, emotions and physical make-up. There is no better formation than a good musical formation; and for this reason there is no more outrageous formation than a bad musical one, which frustrates and distorts the body, which allows the violinist to develop bad, crooked habits, and which imposes a straitjacket, not a discipline, on his impulses and inspiration.

Three
First Facts

A coordination of balance and movement

The body as a whole. It is useful for the violinist to be aware of three stages in developing his technique.

The first, I believe, should be a passive stage. Try to create the vertical awareness of gravity; of hanging; of achieving height by stretching the central diameter as it were to the very top of your head and by allowing your shoulders to 'fall', then your forearms and upper arms. Practise falling at the elbows; allow your hands to fall at the wrists; make your shoulders fall in such a way that they float forwards and backwards, depending on the inclination of your body; hold your wrists at a certain height but at the same time allow your hands and arms to fall, the fingers and elbows pointing down. Keep your neck soft and your head balanced as perfectly as possible, gauging the degree of perfection by the minimum effort required to maintain your head in its upright position.

The next stage is balance. Hold the violin balanced between the thumb and any fingers of your left hand and, at the other extremity, between your collar-bone and chin. Balance the bow in your right hand, so that you can lift it off a string with your hand hanging; your fingers should lie on the bow, with their weight distributed so that the second, and particularly the third and fourth fingers, balance the weight of the stick. Lift the bow from the string, keeping it in an approximately horizontal line with the minimum of pressure on the part of the balancing fingers and with your whole hand still hanging from the wrist. This balance should be maintained in soft, slow motion, and should not inhibit the softness in your neck nor the balance of your body as a whole. You should be poised on your feet, your weight slightly more on your toes – or the balls of your feet – than on your heels.

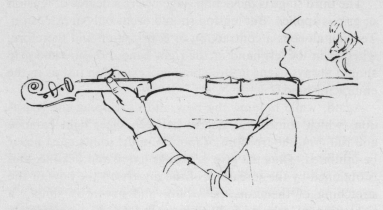

Lifting the head to bring the violin bow up to the horizontal position (see also plate one). Raise the chin above the violin to make way for the new level, otherwise the hand has to fight the head

Before introducing motion with the bow on the violin, it is useful to make swinging circular movements. So put down the instrument and describe circles with both hands in playing positions – that is, with your left hand (as if holding the violin neck) pointing upwards, balanced on top of the wrist as an elongation of the forearm, and with your fingers free to fall; and with your right hand (as if holding the bow) pointing palm downwards, with the fingers and wrist falling and free. With the top of the bent fingers of your left hand describe horizontal circles, as large and smooth as possible; with the drooping right hand make long oval movements, the plane of the oval being between the horizontal and the vertical. During this exercise the rest of your body must contribute to these motions, your head softly balanced on your neck, and all parts – including your waist and hips – moving in coordination.

Then take up the violin and the bow. The same sensations – fluidity, flexibility, balance and softness in the joints –

should obtain, every joint of your body involved to a greater or lesser extent and the balance moving ever so slightly from one foot to the other, depending on where your hands are in the circles they are drawing in the air.

The third stage is the acting stage where a degree of tension or grip is applied. But tension should occur only in extension. Tension alone is a contraction or constriction and therefore, whether in the left hand or the right hand, pressure and grip should always occur in stretching and extension just as in the embracing hold.

Again, while holding the bow and developing the sensations which control the degree between sheer light balance and full grip, the freedom of motion in the joints must never be inhibited. Thus the grip is always living and flexible, and is obtained by the spreading of the fingers on the bow or the stretching of them on the violin, and never by simply a tightening of grip or hold, which, indeed, is a completely false concept.

No matter how firmly you hold the bow and how strongly you can apply the fingers of the left hand to the strings, you must continually go over the check points of your body: neck and head, shoulders, elbows, wrists, knuckles, shoulder blades, chest (for expansion and oxygen), movement of the waist, hips, knees, arches of the feet and toes, and, above all, the full flow throughout these points.

Wrist and fingers. The wrist, of course, is one of the most wonderful joints, in that it can move in all directions. The balance and 'hold' of the bow must obtain equally well in the depressed position of your wrist, in the down-bow – that is, when the bow is drawn with the nut or frog towards the tip or point – as in the course of the up-bow, when the bow is drawn with the wrist in the arched or high position, the hand falling.* In both these positions, and at every point in between, the bow must be both balanced and held, and flexibly so, in such a way that the fingers are allowed the maximum motion in following or directing. The same

*See plates 2 and 3.

obtains in the left hand, which must be free to be pulled or drawn, pushed or thrown, in either direction along the length of the finger-board.

There are two types of motion. The first is when the right fingers on the bow or the left fingers on the finger-board are being pulled by the wrist, and therefore by the knuckles, which are thrown into a depressed position; this occurs on a down-bow (right hand) and when the fingers slide from an upper to a lower position on the finger-board (left hand). The second – again a wrist action – throws the hand into an arched position, as in an up-bow (right hand) or when the fingers slide from a lower to an upper position on the finger-board (left hand).

There is all the difference in the world between this pulling (*drawing* the sound) and this pushing (*throwing* the sound). There is all the difference in the world between the strokes of détaché and those of spiccato (see glossary), which depend entirely on the throwing action, the speed of the strokes, the restriction of the scope. The balance does not come from the violinist actually lifting the bow, but rather from the fact that the bow is kept on the string; it is the speed with which

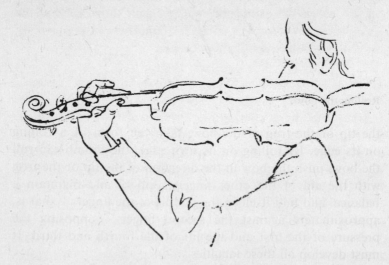

Pulling away with finger and thumb in one position

the bow approaches the string, its weight digging into the string, the speed of the stroke in the confined length, which forces the bow to leave the string at the end of each stroke. The violinist holds the bow *on* the string, but by increasing the speed of the *throw* obliges the bow to leave the string.

Thumb. The role of the thumb against the fingers is, of course, vital to the art of violin playing. And once again utmost flexibility is demanded. The thumb never just clamps with the fingers in position on the bow or the finger-board. It must always be aware of a counter-motion, in either the vertical or the horizontal sense, or of rolling on its edge, of elongating itself by bending or unbending at its joint.† It never simply presses against the finger in a dead, rigid way.

The right thumb touching the underside of the bow-stick remains on the same spot, and the pressures, whether towards

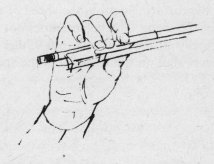

Rolling the bow

the tip or the frog of the bow, take the form of a rolling on its edge. By rolling on its own edge, the thumb can roll the bow, push the bow in the direction of the tip or the frog with the aid of the other fingers, oppose and maintain a balance, and find itself in the middle of the fingers – that is, approximately against the second finger – opposing the pressure of the first and the lift of the fourth and third. It must develop all these faculties.

†See plates 4, 5 and 6.

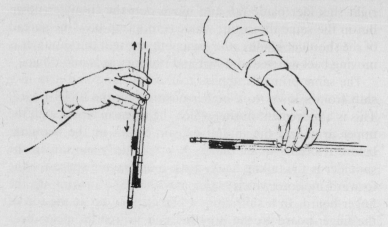

Balanced position in the middle of the bow, with weight on both sides of the thumb

The thumb and fingers must have sufficient scope of action to allow a complete follow-through – similar to the golfer's – in an up-bow stroke, which will carry the bow to the extreme distance it can go in a straight line, on the momentum of its speed.

To illustrate this hand and finger and thumb position, the student may be asked to hold the bow correctly, and then the bow may be pulled in the up-bow direction as far as the fingers, thumb and bent wrist will allow. This gives an example of the extent to which balanced control is demanded, and its scope, for the bow must be balanced at all points along this trajectory.

Shoulder. The more the hand and fingers of the right hand fall away from the wrist, the more relaxed and lower the shoulder and the elbow can be.

The shoulder should be distinguished from the shoulder blades. The shoulder blades expand, as in an embrace, whereas the shoulder itself rolls and falls forwards in the course of a down-bow and backwards and down in the course of an up-bow. Thus, in a down-bow both the shoulder and the right shoulder blade fall and move out, the shoulder down but in the same direction; whereas in an up-bow the spread of the shoulder blade is the same, but above it the shoulder is moving backwards and down and not forwards and down.

The same principle applies to the left hand and arm in a shift from a lower to a higher position on the finger-board. This is a movement during which the forearm closes with the upper arm, and the initiative again comes in the shoulder before it occurs in the hand. A preparatory motion in the shoulder is the falling backwards, thus making space for the forward motion, which anticipates the hand moving up the finger-board. In a shift from a higher position at the top of the finger-board to the opposite end nearer the pegs, near the head of the violin, the preparatory motion is a falling forwards of the shoulder, making space for the motion of the shoulder, which starts to swing back just before the hand and forearm move out and down. The principle is again the opposite motion of the two parts – on the one hand of the shoulder and arm; on the other of the forearm and hand. The V, as it were, opens and closes, but both arms of the V move in opposition to each other.

In playing and practising the violin it is, of course, important to be supremely aware of these minute preparatory and compensating and correlating motions. The delicacy I refer to above begins, naturally, with what we call the 'hold'.

The hold: the left hand

Just as a vibrating bell or a glass can be silenced by clamping down on it, so is violin playing entirely dependent on the absence of any impediment to the free vibrating motion of instrument and player.

Anyone can make the experiment of pressing his left thumb against a left hand finger and of feeling the muscle at the base of the thumb reacting strongly to the degree of pressure. If, however, the experiment is made with the inside side of the thumb nail (on the side of the thumb) pressing against the fingertip, the thumb will be found to be mostly relaxed. It is terribly important in learning to play the violin and in warming up and, in fact, at all times to begin with delicate sensations rather than crude ones.

With reference to the left hand I would at the beginning play a harmonic, that is, a note which is produced by the finger touching the string lightly at given nodular divisions of the string (thus half the string equals the octave, a third equals the fifth, etc) without pressing the string on to the fingerboard. In this position there is virtually no clamping pressure between the thumb and the finger. Then I would proceed to moving the thumb and finger in opposite directions, and finally to applying these opposite directions to thumb and finger without displacing either. The pressure which should be used on the string is not a vertical one, but merely the amount required to keep the finger from sliding on the string.

The more sensitive, soft and pliable the joints and knuckles are, the less pressure will be required to prevent the finger from sliding. This basic motion of applying the finger to the string is coupled, therefore, with the feeling of the thumb and finger moving away from each other, more obviously in the case of the second, third and fourth fingers. This basic action should be done with all fingers on all strings in different positions and should be further coupled with a backward bend of the hand, an opening as it were of the inside wrist. The movements occur simultaneously, the back-bending of the hand together with the motions of the thumb and the playing finger. The further stages involve the left elbow swing towards the player's right combined with the delicate finger pressure as well as a raising of the elbow at the same time to take up the slack caused by the bending back of the hand. We may trace the origin of the movement far back to the shoulder. The motion is accompanied by a relaxation and freeing of the shoulder and finally by a very slight rotation of the body anti-clockwise to meet the elbow (the left elbow swing). The head must also touch the violin very slightly with the violin resting on the collarbone. It is important to raise the elbow and the forearm into the knuckles whilst letting the shoulder drop. In this way the player will encounter no difficulty in moving from low positions to high positions, as he will be continuously on the same level.

This play between thumb and fingers can also be made audible with the particular finger sliding up and down the string in opposition to the thumb movement. The complementary exercises of leaving thumb and finger in one place, the fingers still playing harmonic, while moving in and out with the knuckles to the full extent of both the finger's length and of its folding is a very fine way to develop that minimum pressure which is required to keep the finger from slipping.

The hold: the right hand

The bow should be held at first in the passive stage (see p. 23), so delicately that it does not quite fall from the hand. (Anything slightly less than this hold should allow the bow to drop to the floor.) And with that feeling the bow should be drawn at such a speed over the strings, and with such looseness of wrist and fingers, that it will slide of its own accord in its path or trajectory.

It will slide in the fingers. That is, in the down-bow, the weight of the bow will cause the bow to move away from the fingers, and the fingers will find themselves progressively at an ever higher point of the bow between the frog and the tip. In the up-bow, with a little momentum and slight throw, it is possible to regain the space lost and throw the bow up. This throw depends on which string you are playing – horizontally, as on the A, D and particularly the G string; or nearly vertically, as on the E string. In throwing the bow in the direction of the up-bow, in order to regain the space lost in the down-bow, the fingers find themselves progressively, in different up-bows, nearer and nearer to the frog.

The strong hold of the bow, which evolves in stages from this most delicate hold, is not in order to carry the full

31

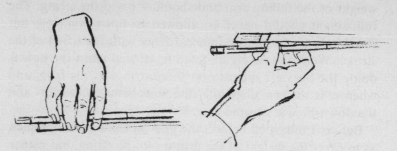

Fingers in medium position, between extremes
(a) viewed from above
(b) viewed from below

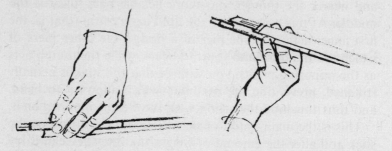

Fingers pointing to heel of bow, extreme position. Fingers and wrist elongated
(a) viewed from above
(b) viewed from below

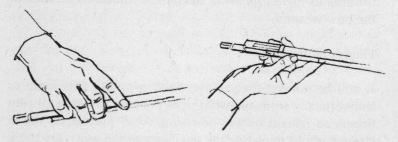

Fingers pointing to tip of bow, extreme position. Thumb and first finger elongated
(a) viewed from above
(b) viewed from below

weight of the falling arm and shoulder on to the string. The full weight should never be allowed to fall completely but should always be gauged in accordance with the speed of the stroke. Weight at its greatest can be carried when the bow is doing the heaviest spiccato on three strings at the frog, and when it is thrown, changing direction between the up- and the down-bow at a rapid rate.

But, as I indicated before, the grip on the bow is not such as to carry the weight of the arm on to the string, but rather to stiffen the stick. This can be readily proved. Move the hand up along the bow to the point where the hold is farthest away from the stiffest part of the bow – which is the frog – and nearer the thinner and more flexible part towards the middle. At this point, when the hold is very firm (that is, the first finger acting as one pier of a bridge, the other piers of which are the third and fourth fingers, while the thumb acts as the opposing pivot), you will see that the stick is actually stiffened, preventing the flexibility which allows it to bend, and thus touching the string with the weight imposed on it.

This is the main object of the strongest grip: to stiffen the stick and alter the amount of weight that the stick can carry without touching the hair and the strings. This was done on the earlier types of bows by the thumb pulling the hair through the medium of the frog and thus increasing the arch of the stick. In those days the stick was still an arch rising towards its highest point in the middle, much as the stick of the bow weapon.

Fingers on the bow

It will be noticed that, as the hand naturally falls more or less vertically from the wrist, it is possible to allow all four fingers to remain on the bow-stick when playing on the G string without impeding the flexibility of the wrist. On the E string, on the other hand, the angle of the stroke is such that if you held all four fingers on the bow, your wrist would be obliged to bend sideways to accommodate the stroke, thus losing its principal action.

It is, therefore, more natural, especially when playing on the E string, to leave only the first and second fingers on the bow; this allows the wrist a freer motion and gives the stroke a wonderful fluency. Of course, when playing on the A and D strings, the adjustment is proportional, involving removal from the bow of the third finger, and eventually the fourth.

Cultivating sensation

It will be understood now how important it is to combine the motions of both arms together, although at first the student will have to try each single motion separately. He must, as soon as possible, add all movements up, so that eventually he uses all parts of his anatomy together, for it is only by engaging the whole body and both arms at once that he will achieve the automatic response, the automatic adjustments which are essential to violin playing. That flow must never be interrupted.

The combination of the motion of the two arms – the left up and down the finger-board, and the right drawing the bow down and up – are possible in an infinity of variations – different rhythms, different lengths and speeds, different weights of the bow and fingers, different distances, covered in different times. There can be one, or one and a half, or two, or three shifts to a bow stroke; there can be the movement of both hands, meeting each other and going away from each other, or moving in the same direction as when the shift in the left hand occurs from the lower to the upper position on a down-bow.

At first it is essential not to worry about actual notes. At this stage it is the sensation which you are cultivating, the feeling of the basic movements.

It is a mistake to assume that violinists play out of tune or inaccurately because they do not hear their sound. Eventually they do become deaf and blind to it, when it cannot be corrected, or when they have given up the hope of correcting it. That, of course, is a negation of violin playing, to stop hearing oneself. But at the beginning it is simply lack of balance and flexibility, and therefore the impossibility of achieving accuracy. After all, how could you measure milli-metres if you only had yard rulers? How could you weigh ounces if you only had hundredweights? And in violin playing intonation, the pitch of a note, its quality, the speed of the vibrato, the bow weights and speeds, the positions on the strings – all these can only be developed through becom-ing aware of the finest measures, those infinitesimal and almost indistinguishable degrees which melt one into the other.

An interesting exercise, and a very useful one for posture, is to stand on your heels, raising your toes off the ground as high as possible. Stand straight. Then bring your body weight as far back as possible on your heels, at which point it will be seen that your chest will rise and come forward to balance your body, and your head will *want* to be erect. Keep this position even when leaning forward. (I believe there is in America a certain brand of shoes called 'Earth Shoes', which deliberately raise the toes above the heels with this in mind.)

Walking is extremely easy when you realize that it depends purely on rising on your toes. If the body is leaning slightly forward (the angle depends on the speed of locomotion), the rise on the left toes allows the body to fall forward on to the next foot. It is an alternate heel-toe movement on each foot, which, at a faster gait, becomes an alternating of toes without the use of the heels, combined with a more angular forward lean of the whole body. There is thus no real effort involved except the rising on each set of toes.

For instance, in running upstairs it is literally only necessary to lean forward and lift each foot alternately off its stair.

In using the body to co-ordinate with the bow-stroke, you must think not only of a horizontal pivoting but must also be aware of the need to balance the extended right arm, on a down-bow, with a slight leaning back and counter-clockwise motion of the body, especially on the G and D strings. When the reverse happens, lean forward as the arm folds inward at the end of the up-bow. If the body does not lean back on a full down-bow, the arm will be inhibited from extending its given length and vice-versa. With these motions, the backwards and forwards leaning, co-ordinated with the down-bow and the up-bow, the violinist will find a far greater freedom and scope in his bowing.

Body stance and bowing

It is important always to practise pianissimo and to allow the strength and power to build up, as control and balance and flexibility of the joints and muscles improve.

I would like to return to the concept of the flow impulse which goes from the tip of the toes to the head, and describe the actual motion, as I feel this represents a conception basic to the down- and the up-bow, which of course are the only two directions in which a bow travels.

No actions occur simultaneously. They always follow on each other and prepare for each other.

In the down-bow, it can be readily understood that the right arm going away from the body either pulls the body around or, if it is a passive stroke, can be thrown out by the body turning clockwise, and imparting that motion to the arm which goes out on the tangent.

Thus the down-bow is associated with a clockwise curving of the body in the waist and, indeed, begins from a first impulse in the toes of the left foot, which push the ground away, so as to induce a clockwise reaction in the body, which turns, mainly at the waist, but also at the hips and in fact throughout the length of the body. This motion, in the course of which the arm's elongation should travel in a natural sequence all the way to the head, which eventually, at the end of the stroke, is allowed to fall to the right, is the ultimate response to that initial push with the big toe and other toes of the left foot.

But just before the head has reached its complete and passive fall, as it is beginning to fall to the right, the violinist should shift his weight slightly to the right foot, and the opposite process begins. The toes of the right foot push the ground away in a direction opposite to the left foot and thus induce a left swing and anti-clockwise turn of the body. This impulse eventually travels to the hand and induces through the shoulder the beginning of an up-bow.

However, at the very beginning of an up-bow, the head is still completing the movement initiated by the down-bow; and at the very beginning of a down-bow, the head is still completing the movement initiated by the up-bow. The impulse is flowing and continuous.

This is a process which should be followed through the various joints of the body – arched feet, ankles, knees, hips, waist, chest, shoulders; through the arms to wrists, hands, fingers. This should sometimes be done quietly. Begin, perhaps, with the down-bow only: turn completely clockwise, and let the head fall to the right over the four strings, and then on each string separately. Begin over the four strings – the lowest, the G, to the highest, the E – and then do it in the opposite direction from the E to the G, which throws the hand up into the air as well as out. Proceed to up-bows only. Finally combine them, and practise doing it more and more perfectly, until the motion is fluid and continuous without a break.

Remember the wrist. At the end of the down-bow the arm is pulling the stroke into a depressed wrist (see p. 25) which eventually throws the hand out, allowing the hand in fact to continue the end of the stroke, and the fingers as well.

The beginning of the stroke should always include a sensation of the hand further falling into the position of the raised wrist, with the shoulder also beginning a new relaxed falling backwards. Again, at the opposite end, as you approach the frog on the up-bow, the hand continues the impulse and, as the shoulder and arm already begin the down-bow, the hand is still continuing the momentum inducing the depressed wrist, which goes on to depress a little more yet at the beginning of the down-bow.

The head does not always move towards the left in an up-bow, but depends on the shortness and speed of the stroke, as well as on the particular string crossing, whether clockwise or anti-clockwise. The shorter the stroke, the quicker the opposite motions coincide with the still continuing stroke. In other words, the shortest stroke is really the same as the very end of a long stroke where the motions are diametrically opposed – the motion of stroke by that time is only momentum and impulse, which are already the opposing motion.

Take the matter of string crossings. Draw at the tip a down-bow on the G string and an up-bow on the open E string. Do this in fairly rapid succession, allowing the head to adjust and move freely. You will notice that, on the up-bow, the head does in fact move to the left and, on the down-bow, to the right. If, however, you do the anti-clockwise rotation, which is down-bow on the E string and up-bow on the G, you will notice that the natural motion induces the head to go to the left on the down-bow and to fall to the right on the up-bow. This is, in fact, a very good exercise to loosen the neck and to allow the head to balance freely without tension on the vertebrae.

Warming up

One of the most important warming-up exercises is the whole body motion, which consists of the following four variations. The first is a swinging rotation of the body from right to left, impelled by the right toes combined with a long up-bow. The impetus of this movement should go into the elbow; into the head which should roll over on to its left ear; into the fingers that hold the bow which should go into the position in which they are pulled by the bow going into an extreme up-bow position. The right hand should end beyond the violin and the player's head. The swing should begin with a feeling of complete relaxation in the fingers of the right hand allowing the bow to drop from the wrist and the fingers. The left elbow should likewise swing freely. This motion can be combined with the fingers on the violin sliding from the first position to say the tenth position and again going from the tenth position to the first.

The second exercise is also an up-bow, but this time a very short and fast one with the body rotating from left to right which, together with the violin, moves against the direction of the bow. This, of course, shortens the time and the stroke.

The next two exercises concern the down-bow which we begin beyond the violin and beyond our left ear in the air and in which we rotate from left to right. We end beyond the tip of the bow with the bow in a dropped wrist and hand position.

The same holds true for these down-bow exercises where the head must fall on to its right side, the left elbow hanging like a pendulum following the motion, the shoulders equally relaxed; in fact, every part of the body participating in the motion and combined with the left hand sliding up or sliding down the fingerboard.

The fourth exercise is a fast down-bow in which the same principles hold, but the body rotates anti-clockwise against the down-bow direction.

In the swinging action of the body when the right toes swing the body on to the left leg, it is our left heel which sends the body rotating back again.

It is important to separate the different elements and parts of elements and at the same time it is important to gather them* together in one all-embracing activity. For instance, the right shoulder-blade is in a way quite independent from the right shoulder; the shoulder-blade falls forward in the course of the strokes, while the shoulder itself floats. Once these movements are caught they are really most enjoyable and practice no longer becomes a chore, but a delight.

Gravity is one of our most important allies. We naturally assume that in a down-bow the right arm falls, particularly on the E string, but we forget to what extent gravity helps us even in the up-bow in terms of the elbow and the arm, and the shoulder-blade which also fall in a controlled and delicate way. Above all, bowing is a floating sensation.

* i.e. the various muscle groups and sections of our limbs.

Four
Technique

Some aims to follow

The violinist must never give up his vision of effortless
perfection. However insuperable and non-yielding the difficulty may appear, however long the process of analysis and
discovery may take, remember that in fact the obstacles are
but 'paper tigers', as the Chinese would say.

The violinist must develop:

1. A sense of extended, embraced, open, yet contained *space*.
2. A natural *co-ordination* (for example, co-ordination of
   movement and breathing).
3. A feeling in body, limbs and fingers of exquisite and
   precise *balance*.
4. A fine sense of *weight*. The weight of limbs, arms, hands
   and fingers must change. For instance, weight must be
   more when extended than when bent, when horizontal
   than when vertical, when supported than when hanging;
   and also when speed of motion is too slow to generate
   momentum or when a movement is natural and perfect in
   shape.
5. A fine sense of speeds and ranges of *oscillation* – from
   vibration to pendulum, as of circular and elliptical
   motions.
6. An *awareness* of that particular point along the course of
   an ellipse or circle at which the active impulse occurs.
   This usually happens as a reinforcement of a gravitational
   fall. It is also necessary to develop an awareness of the
   passive momentum which follows the active impulse.
   These sensations are not black and white – but rather a

taking over one from another; the active grows out of the passive, just as the passive ebbs when the apex of the initiative is reached.

7. *Some general points:*

Always remember to play with balance not grip. The touch, the feel of strings, violin neck, chin-rest and bow, should always be the *least* possible.

Release effort completely (or almost) between each effort.

Be aware of *continuous* motion. Create circles or ellipses. Continuous motion, with one impetus, takes in a complete rotation of: pendel (pendulum); swing; oscillation.

Whenever tired, even if after only thirty seconds, let your arms drop and allow the violin to drop to its natural angle when held only with weight of your head. Alternatively, put your tools down and lie on the floor for a few moments.

While performing let your mind think slightly ahead; do not allow any reflex to take place in limbs or fingers, for they must act *not a moment* before the appointed time. The wonderful suddenness of certain Japanese movements derives from this passive attitude of the physical body which, however much the mind calculates, simply takes no part in any mental deliberations, but acts only at the *right* instant and not a split fraction of a second before.

In every completed movement (i.e. return to your beginning position) be aware of strong (active) impetus and soft (passive) momentum (see 6, above). Learn to recognize the interchange of both.

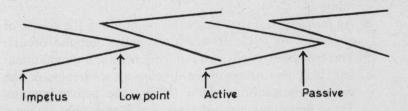

Impetus   Low point   Active   Passive

Thus, in the repeated body rotation (to be described below), with an up-bow on either left or right hand rotation (i.e. two to one – two rotations to one stroke – or one to two – one stroke to two rotations), beginning on either an anti-clockwise or a clockwise swing, be aware that the direction of the swing occurring on the stroke is a leading one, an active one. The opposite can be tried as well, i.e. a down-bow in the air can be made into an active motion, with the actual stroke a passive reflex action. I say this because I believe that it is important, as in life itself, to realize the alternation of light and dark, hard and soft, inhalation and exhalation.

In pendel motion, consider not the circle but the return to the gravitational mean, the middle-point of repose.

The bow is breath and, like the singer's breath, must be husbanded, equitably apportioned to each section and each note.

Some common faults

The violinist's enemy is any tightness of hold, whether of fingers, hands, arms, shoulders, head, neck, chest (right or left side), shoulder-blades, waist, hips, knees, ankles or feet; in fact, any impediment whatsoever to the instantaneous translation of a total impulse – emotional, physical, spiritual or intellectual – into the reality of sound. These impediments may be due to dietary deficiencies, bad posture, poor circulation, over-eating, stress, fear, tension and bad violinistic habits. Some such bad habits are listed below:

Head	tilted
	cheek on chinrest
	too much pressure on chinrest
Shoulders	raised
Left arm	elbow resting on ribs
	wrist 'in' or 'out'
	fingers too 'low' in relation to fingerboard

          thumb striding above fingerboard or under neck

          neck resting in bottom of space between thumb
            and first fingers

          'gripping' of neck

          line of knuckles going out at right angles from
            fingerboard

          violin pointing to ground

Right arm lack of action in elbow (bowing from the shoulder)
            in détaché

          lack of vertical action in elbow (elevation)

          stiffness in wrist

          rigid thumb

          fingers too tightly together

          bow strokes *not* in line with bridge

Body   rigid or too willowy

Feet   together or too far apart

Oscillating exercises

Lie on your back with your arms extended behind your head.
Bring both legs up, swing them over your head, until you
touch the floor with your toes behind your head (plough pose).
A yoga shoulder-stand is the inverted body in a vertical
position, supported on the back of the neck and the upper
arms on the floor, with palms against the back. This can be
achieved from the plough pose. Now swing your body, from
neck and hips, over your head, while your legs balance in the
opposite direction, and vice versa. This is an oscillation.

Simple oscillation In a standing position (arms hanging at
your sides) oscillate between toes and heels. As your body
bends backwards and your shoulders and head fall backwards
you should move on to your toes. As your body bends
forwards and your shoulders and head fall forwards, you
should move on to your heels. Also do this exercise from side
to side, shoulder and head falling alternately on each side.

Horizontal oscillations (*or rotations*) Do these exercises bare-
foot. In a standing position, rotate your body, the impulse
coming from your feet. By pushing backwards with the
left foot and forwards with the right, the body is thrown
into a clockwise rotation. Pushing backwards with right foot
and forward with left returns the body in an anti-clockwise
rotation. You will notice that the impulse seems to begin with
the heel of one foot and the ball (behind toes) of the other.
However, one can trace its start to yet an earlier preparatory
motion in the pushing back of the knee from a slightly bent
and a relaxed position – an action which flows into the heel.

Allow the rotation to go through the knees into the hips,
then into the waist, which movement will throw the arms
flying to one side. Begin an opposite movement when your
arms and hands arrive at their maximum position, hitting
behind your body: this will give extra motion to your shoulder. Allow your head to rotate as well, and allow your body
rotations to include sideways roll. Then raise your hands
and arms to a horizontal position, and higher, and allow
them to join in the circular movements.

The heel (say the right), in pushing the ground back,
originates the swing, which travels spirally all the way to the
head. Initially it leaves the right-hand side of the body (chest,
shoulder blade) behind. This is a wonderful sensation, which
allows the right shoulder to remain relaxed and low, and gives
a great feeling of space, increasing the lung and breathing
capacity.

Naturally, a body swing or oscillation can also originate
from an upper part of the body – not necessarily from the
feet, but from the swing of an arm, or arms, shoulder or
head. In body swings it is possible to give an impetus
preparatory to each change of direction, particularly when
throwing the arms and hands against the body, which action
finishes the swing while feet begin the return swing. In this
case it is more like an oscillation than a pendel, for it is a
horizontal motion. Even so there is a quiet middle-point.
Walking is a similar swing and enjoys equal impetus on left
and right. Depending on speed, the body should lean

slightly forward to catch the next step. In walking we should naturally, in addition to swinging, fall forward from each rise from the left or right toes.

Whole body swing

1. The first part of the stroke is with an anti-clockwise motion of your whole body, rotation to the left. The second part rotates in the opposite direction to *meet* the bow, your hand continuing into the extreme down-bow position at the end of the up-bow stroke in the air beyond the violin.
2. For whole down-bow strokes, begin the first part of the stroke with a clockwise rotation at your waist, initiated with your feet. Then begin opposite, alternate rotation somewhere along the stroke, ending the down-bow stroke beyond the violin in the air with falling hand.

The last note of the stroke already

changes the body direction, continuing in the same direction for the first notes of the following stroke

also beginning with the upper notes.

Part One: The Violin
Exercises with violin and bow

After practising my preliminary exercises you may feel like resting on the floor; if so, *do* so. Alternatively, you can take up your instrument. Hold the violin and bow with *minimum* strength – a hold derived from *balance*, not from *grip* – and with all joints (fingers, wrists, arms, elbows, shoulders) free and soft. (See page 25).

Co-ordinating left and right arms and hands, make a right-hand, clockwise rotation with the body, together with a down-bow, coming down from above the violin and continuing beyond it. At the same time with left hand play

on A and D strings ♭C – ♭C, octave jumps. This does *not* have to be accurate. In fact, any concern with accuracy at this stage should be forgotten; we are concerned with basic co-ordinations of gross movements. This motion may be combined with an exhalation.

The same principle should be applied to an up-bow, i.e. swing to the left, exhale, etc.

It will be noticed that when the V bow (up-bow) is played on G string, the swing is horizontal, whereas on E string the movement includes a vertical component. The ⊓ bow (down-bow) differs in the same respect, whether on G or E or any intermediate string.

Now do the down-bow to a left-hand, anti-clockwise body swing. The stroke is fast as the body moves in the opposite direction. Then do the same with the up-bow. The left hand slides up or down the fingerboard with each stroke, as you decide. Take long strokes sometimes. Also take one bounce, then two, or three or more bounces to a stroke. Of course, these combined movements of body and right arm

46

Plate 1. Natural hang of the violin when head weight alone holds it, without shoulder or hand.

Many violinists believe that the violin should remain horizontal even when the left arm hangs. This, I feel, is wrong, because it requires a raising and tensing of the shoulder and neck muscles. (See also drawing on p. 24.)

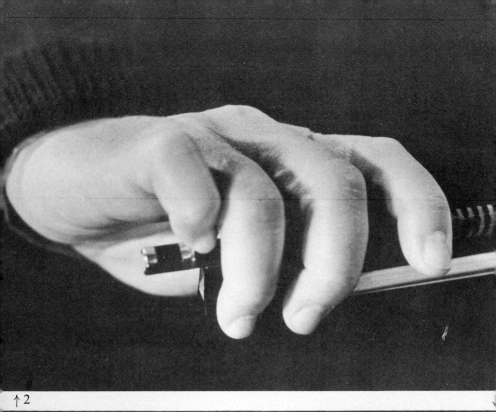

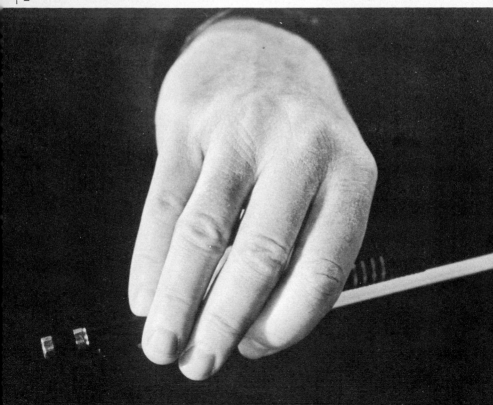

bow strokes are in fact crude, because the actual relationship of body rotation to stroke is not simultaneous in either parallel *or* opposite directions.

With body rotation, practise anticipating changes of bow direction on whole strokes, ∨ ⊓ – ∨ ⊓ bow, leaving string or strings (if double-stops) after each stroke, whether long or short smooth détaché or martelé on strings.

Practise also with three body rotations to one détaché stroke, thus:

The three rotations to each single stroke are: **(1)** opposite to stroke, short (fast); **(2)** parallel with stroke, long (slow); **(3)** opposite to stroke, again short.

Practise with **(1)** long; **(2)** short (as bow approaches point); up-bow begins with a short **(3)**; continues with a long **(4)**; and short **(5)** as bow approaches frog. Down-bow begins with a short **(6)**; continues with a long **(7)**; then short **(8)** as bow reaches point for up-bow, on short **(9)**, etc. etc.

After practising three to one (three shiftings simultaneously with three rotations to one whole stroke), do four to one:

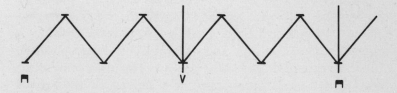

and vice versa, beginning on an upper octave.

In practising the following patterns, adjust arm levels to alternating levels of double stops.

Plate 2. The bow hand in the extreme up-bow position

Plate 3. The bow hand in the extreme down-bow position

Part One: The Violin

In the three to one, add exercise:

Play the above rhythm at the frog, the remainder of this stroke in the air.

Do this on the same string, as well as with the two notes on a different string each. Repeat the same exercise on different parts of the bow, in the same rhythm but beginning with a down- instead of an up-bow.

The left hand

During our three body rotations to one stroke (see above), the left hand should play on A and D strings (or on any other two adjacent strings) with first and third fingers *playing thirds*.

Or begin with

with second and fourth fingers.

The left elbow pendel (swing) should co-ordinate *not* with bow-stroke, but with left hand shift. In one pattern, the elbow approaches the body-side as the higher position is approached, and swings away towards the lower position. In the other pattern, the elbow goes away from the body as the higher position is approached. On the whole the second pattern is better suited to shorter shifts and to *ends* of shifts.

In practising shiftings it is good to prepare a change from a low position to a higher position by first 'making space'. Allow your left shoulder to fall backwards preparatory to a shift. The shift then brings your shoulder slightly forward, moving in the opposite direction, as if to meet your hand. To prepare a shift from a high position to a low one, the opposite takes place: the shoulder first falls forward in preparation, then, simultaneously with the shift, moves back in an opposite motion to the hand, going *away* from the hand.

The left elbow should pendel (swing) *towards* the body when the body rotates to the left, and away from the body when the rotation is to the right. This should happen regardless of whether the above exercise begins with an up-bow or a down-bow, i.e. regardless of whether the left hand is in the lower or the upper position. Thus:

1. *In an up-bow:*
Elbow away from side: right rotation.
Elbow touching side: left rotation.
In the returning down-bow, beginning with higher ˙octave thirds: the opposite sequence.

2. *In a down-bow* (beginning as above on a lower note):
Elbow swings towards side: left rotation.
Elbow away from side: right rotation.
The octave pattern between should be continued all the way up the fingerboard on all strings, as far as

on A and D strings.

These exercises produce a flowing integration of left and right arms and elbows, together with the body swing.

In fact, in the higher positions, the 'opposite' swing (as in (2), above) – the pivoting motion, when the elbow swings

49

away from the body as the head goes into a higher position – will be found the more natural. There is a last stretch of fingerboard in the highest positions which depends especially on finger extensions.

On the A and D strings

in using the first and third fingers in the higher positions, this finger stretch at the top of the shift is evident. But when using the second and fourth fingers, the left arm must come both higher and further around, because the little finger (the fourth finger) has no extension when coupled with the second finger and when playing on a lower string.

The following exercises for short strokes and, later, long strokes should be done to left-hand patterns:

(a) Slides on *all* strings.
    With any interval, and between any positions, and with any and every pair of fingers, in fourths, seconds, octaves, tenths, etc.

(b) Also on thirds with fingers 2 and 4.
    And on string crossings (at first between neighbouring strings).

50

(c) Also on finger fall.

Left hand exercises

Finger exercises. The violin should be held in such a way that the left hand is well above the string with the forearm continuing in a more or less straight line, from the elbow to the knuckles at the base of the fingers.

A very good exercise is the vertical one, thumb and fingers at one spot, and the forearm then raised at the elbow without moving the fingers. Another good exercise is rolling the violin between thumb and fingers.* And a third is the opposite motion of thumb and finger or fingers.

And, of course, there is the basic motion of the left hand on the finger-board, which is either the pulling by the arm of the fingers, along the string towards the bridge (into a depressed wrist) or the throwing of the fingers, along the string towards the head (from an arched wrist). These hand movements on the finger-board correspond to those on the bow (see p. 25). A normal shift may use both, beginning with the pulling and ending with the throwing, in the same way and observing the same principle as the right hand.

To develop finger stretch, it is important to concentrate not only on the fingers, but on the spread of the knuckles. A very good exercise is to spread 'reluctant' fingers by spreading the knuckles apart rather than the fingers. The fingers will thus roll over on their sides opposite each other, hardly moving from their notes (a half tone apart), while the knuckles attempt to pull them apart.

*See plates 4 and 5.

Part One: The Violin

The following finger exercises are designed to develop flexibility, strength and accuracy, and are of course particularly useful for vibrato and shifting.

With a finger on each string in a low, a middle and a high position, and with your thumb touching the left side of the neck with the softest part of its upper joint, *pull* (away, towards the head of the violin) extending your fingers and wrist, without any finger actually moving away from its given note. *Maintaining* this pull, bend your fingers, thus bringing your hand and wrist back to their normal aspect. Slowly release the bent fingers, always maintaining the same directional *pull*. Repeat.

Push your hand (i.e. wrist and fingers) towards you, folding your fingers to their most compressed condition. *Maintaining* this push, and with no finger moving from its note, forcibly, slowly, elongate (unfold) and extend fingers and wrist. Then slowly release, returning to original aspect.

These are resistance exercises opposing arm-to-wrist finger motions or pressures.

Next, with your thumb remaining on one spot and itself pushing towards the violin head, simultaneously slide a finger to as high a position as it can reach without the thumb abandoning its spot. This can be done with the aid of the wrist. The wrist can either move in the same direction as the finger or in the opposite direction (bending back) whilst the forearm moves forward.

Now the opposite exercise. The thumb remains in the same place, pushing in the direction of the bridge of the violin, while the finger slides to the lowest possible position. First do this with the wrist (and hand) moving, bending back in same direction as the finger; then in the opposite direction with the forearm moving back in the same direction as the finger.

Shifting we have already covered, but the above exercises yield music when they are applied to arpeggios and scales with one finger. Later they can be carried out also in thirds and all other intervals, on one or (when using double stops) on two strings.

52

Choosing one of your four fingers, play a scale or arpeggio in the two following ways on the G string:

shiftings up and down

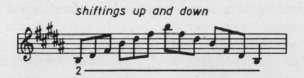

First, push with your forearm into folding fingers for each note on the way up. Relax between moves. Pull with your forearm from extended fingers for each note on way down. Relax back into the middle normal position of knuckles and fingers between notes.

Secondly, make the finger itself take the initiative. Extend the finger alone, from say B to D sharp. Then pull hand, wrist and forearm to the finger, into a folded position. The same should be repeated for each note on the way up. To go down, from say top B to F sharp, begin by folding the finger back upon itself. Then, on F sharp, it should push itself into an extended position, bringing back with this effort hand, wrist and forearm, ready to repeat the same procedure for the next note – D sharp.

This arpeggio, or chromatic scale, should be done on all four strings with each finger.

Vibrato. With the hand in the third position, the thumb remaining on its spot, oscillate between third and first positions with each finger in turn touching the string lightly and with rhythmic accent on the note in the *first* position. First do this slowly, then fast. When playing these one-finger oscillations fast, perform in the first position, thumb and arm remaining in the third position on $\frac{1}{2}$ tone (or whole tone) oscillations, simple vibrato. This is wonderful for the wrist. It balances two directions of oscillations – away and towards.*

*The inspiration for this vibrato exercise is contained in Louis Kierman's *Practising the Viola*, published by Keldon Publications, 1343 Amalfi Drive, Pacific Palisades, California 90272. This is an excellent handbook.

Trills. Always concentrate on lift. Thus the accent should be in the fingers of the left hand, not on the coming-down note, but on fast, sudden, light lift.

In the following examples the accent > refers *not* to sound or to bow, but purely to lift of finger.

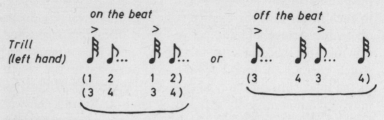

These should be practised between all finger pairs and in double stops.

Lifting of fingers may be combined either with the wrist bending in, or, as a different exercise, with the wrist bending out, in all positions and on all strings.

I believe all trill exercises should be practised in one of the basic combinations* always alternating the lift and fall of each finger and each pair of fingers. Progress will thus be much quicker, and the fingers strengthened much more quickly without the danger of that seizure which is so often the case with a violinist's trill.

*See p. 55: the three basic combinations of double stops.

Further left hand development

I call this the 'pussy-foot' technique. Never smack a finger down on the fingerboard; let each finger fall with its own weight on to the string. This will not be sufficient to depress the string on to the fingerboard. Upon contact with the string, push the string to the fingerboard. There are thus two sections to each finger-fall, the passive (when the finger merely drops on to the string) and the active (when the string is pushed down). This becomes, in fact, one uninterrupted motion, which carries no sound from the finger hitting the string or the finger hitting the fingerboard. The muscles of the arm must remain completely soft; check continually and you will soon be able to feel this without actually touching the upper arm muscles. The hand rises slightly on to the finger as full pressure (weight) is applied on each note in turn.

Use the 'pussy-foot' technique on one finger at a time, barely releasing the string between each pressure. Pressure means a simultaneous lifting (through the finger alone) of the hand knuckles. Then alternate between two fingers. This is a complementary exercise to lifting (trill) and should be done immediately afterwards.

As you work with one finger, allow the other three fingers to remain on the strings in either of two positions or a combination of these – either resting on the strings, as in natural harmonies, or holding the notes down with the strings touching the fingerboard.

Double stops

Although at first the student violinist will use one finger of the left hand at a time, he should soon begin double stops. There are three basic combinations of double stops. The best one to begin with is thirds, for these put the hand in a good position. Work with two pairs of thirds which may be alternated, pairing the first and third fingers, and the second and fourth. It is a good idea in practising to raise the lower pair while applying the upper pair – raising one and three while applying two and four, and *vice versa*. This gives the hand double the exercise and prevents any congealing of muscles into rigid and tense positions.

The second pair of double stops consists of the first and second fingers, alternating with the third and fourth fingers. These can be practised in the intervals of fourths and sixths, or thirds with the fingers in the stretched positions. Then, thirdly, the second and third fingers, alternating with the first and fourth, should practise in the intervals of sixths with tenths or fourths, with the unison, or a minor second instead of the unison, with the fourth finger on a C on the D string, and the first finger on a B on the A string, the second and third fingers playing in their turn the D and A respectively.

Chords

In chordal writing the violinist has an additional problem, for he must play the notes of the chord and must also decide which of those notes are the most important melodically. These notes must never be lost hold of, but must remain in the ear from the beginning of the bar. At the same time the player must decide on the length of the subsidiary notes of the chord. And sometimes he must compromise with what is or is not possible, but on the whole the works are written for performance and they are indeed more than possible; they are written with specific fingerings in mind.

I am not in favour of inverted chord playing, that is beginning a chord from the upper note, because I feel that if it is the lower note that is important it should be heard on the beat. Instead I believe that it is just possible to play the note on the beat, to follow it with the other note of the chord including notes on all the other strings, and return to the lowest string, the G string, with hardly a break, quickly enough to give the illusion of the lower note in this instance having been continuous, unbroken.

When practising

When playing scales upwards with fingering 1, 2, 3, 4 re-

56

peated on successive strings, the left elbow, forearm and wrist must come in towards the side to help the fourth finger, which is the shortest finger. The same auxiliary motion takes place on downwards scales each time the fourth finger plays.

Very often violinists allow all open strings to sound between notes on two strings played with the same finger. This is a very bad habit.

A good exercise is to play the following with the same finger:

across fingerboard

Or, beginning with D or G string, play four notes (fifths) on four strings with your fourth finger. Work this same exercise in all positions with all fingers. It will be found that with the aid of the first joint the finger can roll on to or away from a string, redirecting its normal position on each string without interrupted sound.

Practise this same exercise with double stops.

A good finger exercise is to take a double stop (any one) and force the strings apart with two fingers and bring them closer together alternately.

Right hand finger exercises

To strengthen the fingers it is useful to hold the bow vertically in the air and to move it, at first very slightly, describing with the tip a very small section of an arc, with your fingers only gradually increasing the arc with arm rotation. Do the same starting horizontally. Hold the bow horizontally and with a loose wrist shake your hand up and down. Your hold on the bow should be very light – just sufficient not to drop it.

Hold the bow vertically and, with loose shake of your wrist, move it vertically up and down into your fingers.

Then, holding the bow horizontally, combine these various movements into circles, both clockwise and anti-clockwise. Now do the same with the bow nearer to the vertical angle.

The up-bow

To analyse the up-bow it is useful to remember that the centre of motive power, as you move over the length of the bow from tip to frog, passes from your arm to your shoulder, your shoulder gradually taking on initiative as your arm (forearm as well as upper arm) passively surrenders it. During the last portion of an up-bow, the shoulder (limp, almost passive) should not stop, but continue pushing, floating, hanging. Nor should you forget that, as the wrist bends as the hand falls when the frog is approached, the shoulder and upper arm must actually travel a longer distance than the bow travels on the string. The very slight rotation of the bow in the dropped wrist position is in reality only the natural fall of the bow in the direction of the upright position, i.e. the bow with hair flat on the string.

In approaching the frog on an up-bow, your fingers (including the fourth – little – finger) should lie on the bow sufficiently firmly to carry some of the weight of the bow at the frog and to lift the bow off a string on a particular string plane if the forearm is slightly lifted. It is generally accepted that in a down-bow the arm falls (although this is not necessarily true when playing on the G string); but it is overlooked that there is a *falling* component in the up-bow, namely, when nearing the frog, the elbow and the shoulder-blade make a motion, *slight* but definitely present.

To take advantage of this very slight falling of the elbow towards the end of an up-bow, the plane of the upper arm and forearm must be neither too high nor too low, and must be adjustable.

In ff, an up-bow stroke, you should feel, in the lower half, as if resistance of string is actually pushing your shoulder-blade back, with your forearm and upper arm passive, whilst the motive power is transferred all the way back into your shoulder-blade. It is the shoulder-blade which supports and pushes the latter section of stroke.

A very useful approach to develop lightness and balance in the right hand

In this approach,* the bow speed at the approach to a change of direction of stroke is maintained (or reduced) by a whole hand movement. It involves a large wrist action, mostly rotational, which – after raising the wrist, thus allowing the hand to fall in the approach to the frog – follows through with ring-hold (thumb and second finger) and lightest touch until the hand is tilted on the little finger side, possibly with the little finger balancing the bow weight and the wrist somewhat depressed, with the arm already pulling the down-bow. This is not a last-minute adjustment, but a gentle, soft and continuous motion, always in balance, with no momentum at slower speeds; and it can begin almost at the point of the bow.

The opposite happens in the change from down-bow to up-bow at the upper part of the bow. With a large motion from a lower wrist to a higher wrist, the whole hand describes a half circle, from the tilt of the hand on the first finger side to somewhat less, perhaps, on the up-bow. At the beginning of the up-bow, the first and second fingers, still lying on the first finger side, should elongate from the bent position at the end of the down-bow. A very smooth and continuous action is the object, with the bow leaning backwards on hair at the end of the down-bow, allowing for crescendo if necessary.

Pressure is developed at the end of the down-bow, whilst lightness and the carrying-of bow is developed at the end of the up-bow on slow bows. When using fast, long bows, lightness is necessary along the whole course.

*I owe the above to an exposition by Michael Schwalbé.

Practise these exercises on three and four strings at the frog:

Then practise vice versa (up-bow on the E string). Then again at point, the down-bow beginning on the G string.

Co-ordination with the left hand. In bowing exercises it is important to cultivate a real distinction between carrying, smooth, continuous, floating feelings and the degree of pressure required. Pressure is independent of floating, and one sensation must not affect the other.

It is necessary to work on the chromatic scales with the left hand co-ordinating with the right hand portato. In upwards scales your left hand and shoulder should lean on the notes thus:

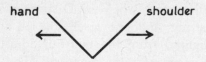

Then, relaxing between each note, move into the opposite condition.

In downwards scales your left hand and shoulder should lean on the notes in an upward direction thus:

Then relax into the opposite condition *between* notes, i.e. directing shifts.

The respective shoulder always leads, however imperceptibly, whether in left hand shifting or bowing. For instance, in the down-bow the weight or pull of the shoulder is the beginning of the stroke and before the bow actually moves a preparatory sensation should occur all the way back to the shoulder. The fingers, including the knuckles and wrist, submit to this impulse. The opposite occurs before the fingers yield in the up-bow, and eventually both arms are softly exercised, as well as the body, on octave jumps, scales, double stops and arpeggios.

Different levels of left and right arms

In practising the following patterns, adjust arm levels to alternating levels of double stops:

These two examples show the left arm closer to the body on the major second, when the D string is more depressed than the A string; and, conversely, the left arm swings away (however slightly) from the body to adjust to the octave when the A string is more depressed. The bowing adjusts correspondingly. These exercises should be practised *pp*, in higher positions as well, and on the three pairs of strings.

Play these intervals in the ♪ ♪ rhythm at the frog,

the remainder of this stroke in the air.

Do this on the same string, as well as with the two notes on a different string each. Repeat the same exercise on different parts of the bow, in the same rhythm but beginning with a down- instead of an up-bow.

61

Follow-through exercises. Your whole body should turn at least half-circle, looking down anti-clockwise for the up-bow, and clockwise for the down-bow. Next stage: with the up-bow, begin on an anti-clockwise turn, and end on a clockwise turn, inducing the down-bow response, connecting at your shoulder in the air. Reverse this for the down-bow, beginning clockwise and ending anti-clockwise, thus inducing an up-bow response.

Bowing exercises. Accuracy of intonation, accuracy and judgement of distance in bowing, will only come once the distances have been conquered in their extreme lengths, and once sensitivity has been developed – but not before. That is why I am always anxious to see that the whole bow is used and that as soon as possible the student, in using one finger at a time, jumps the distance of two octaves on the violin strings. Beginning with the A on the G string with the first finger, he should reach the A two octaves above, still on the G string, equivalent to the first A on the E string. And so on and so forth, with each finger on each string.

As for the development of sensitivity, I cannot stress sufficiently the importance of avoiding clamps and holds. To this end it is very useful, in practising with the bow, to practise with only the second, that is the middle, finger and the fourth finger poised on top (or nearly on top) of the stick, with no other fingers touching the bow. This will make a very soft sound and the player will perhaps lose his bow a few times but it encourages a very delicate hold of the bow and the obligation of the whole arm, the wrist, the whole complex to move along with the hand more or less in one piece, and to change levels as one piece depending on the different strings played.

Three basic strokes in violin playing

There are three basic strokes which – when variously combined, and when practised both on and off the string (i.e. in all bow divisions with various weights and pressures) and with one, two and more repeats on one stroke, and with short pauses between strokes, and at various speeds – account for all violin bowing. They are:

1. *Short martelé* in which the fingers and hand take the initiative; this stroke is *thrown* rather than pulled. At the frog the elbow must rise on a down-bow to make vertical space for the falling hand (from the wrist), otherwise a scratchy sound results at the end of the down-stroke. The stroke is longish and the forearm or shoulder motion is shorter than the stroke.

2. *Short détaché* (the opposite) in which the stroke (the actual distance the bow travels on the string) is shorter and the shoulder or forearm motion is longer. These smooth strokes give uninterrupted sound. Holding the bow very delicately and doing short body rotations in the opposite direction to the strokes (this also applies to the short martelé), maximum movement is generated in the limb, in the wrist, in the fingers and in the thumb, whilst the bow travels a minimal distance. A light hold ensures that balance is correct and all joints are ready to give. A further exercise involves the same motions with more weight allowed to fall on the bow, using all fingers on the bow.

To develop the lightest possible grip on the bow, imagine that you are practising the opposite movement to a hold – that the fingers and thumb are going away from the stick – almost, but not quite, of course, dropping the stick. This will give you a wonderful sensation of free flight. It is as much an attitude to life in general as an ancient moral precept, or so I believe, that, as soon as we try to hold tightly on to possessions, position, other people, we lose our freedom, inspiration and sensitivity; we can no longer react with compassion, nor create.

3. *Smooth strokes,* rather slowish or interrupted, with minimum motion in fingers and wrist, and travel distance *equal* and proportional between bow and string on the one hand and forearm or shoulder on the other, as the case may be.

Our third variety of stroke involves *no* momentum. Although body rotation may be used, it is quiet, slow and does not build up any impetus. It is *very* important to practise this stroke with the fingers merely resting on the bow and the pp arm floating. This stroke is an antidote to the other two and is essential for long, slow strokes in p and f, and for staccato as well as for ricochet. Staccato requires a delicately balanced hold with *no* change in overall détaché positions, relative speeds, floating arm, or location of initiative, but loose, minute and delicate *tremolo* in the forearm, as fast as possible.

Exercises in these areas should be done lifting the bow off the string between each stroke, always together with body rotation (oscillation). When martelé motion (our first example) is used to produce a détaché, this results in a fast smooth détaché. At the frog the particular martelé motion of slightly raising the elbow on a down-bow is visible as the loose wrist is shaken at higher speeds. When the bow is lifted between strokes, practise strokes as either martelé (beginning with incisive accent), soft bounce, or brush stroke (smooth attack, or rather approach). Spiccato, for instance, is the result of a fast détaché played with the bow flattish and a somewhat lowered elbow, with the bow held *into* the string and played with a fast almost martelé motion. I say *almost* because there is still a trace of a détaché pull at the very beginning of each stroke. The fast détaché at the frog should be done with a high elbow in order to permit the free wrist-stroke to assume a more horizontal, rather than a vertical plane. Lowering the elbow and increasing the détaché component of stroke will bring about a heavy frog and resonant spiccato.

Martelé and détaché should be practised on various portions of the bow and on *whole* bow strokes. All fast initial martelé and slow continuation détaché combinations in one stroke are not only possible but an essential part of the violinist's equipment.

Bowing pressures

It is equally important to experiment with different combinations of fingers and to find out how, for instance, the angled pressure of the first finger away from the bridge is balanced by the thumb rolling the bow in the opposite direction; how the angle pressure is achieved between the first and third fingers or, often in the upper part of the bow, between the first and second fingers; and how when the first finger pressure is towards the bridge the thumb rotates the bow again in the opposite direction. The thumb must be free to be or not to be, to exert or not to exert a little pressure, to roll the stick and to roll on its own edge. It must be extremely sensitive. Nor can the muscles at the base of the thumb between the thumb and the base of the first finger be allowed to remain tight.

In fact, the thumb of the right hand is as often as not a pivot on which the bow rests.

It is important to remember that reactions in the fingers of the right hand must be very sensitive and faster than any actual stroke for they are there to modify the stroke. If they are slower than a bow stroke the whole of the bow becomes what we might call a club hold, for we cannot modify within the stroke. The whole quality of violin playing depends on constant and subtle modification of the stroke to give it expression and colour.

In this connection it is very useful to practise on one stroke a delicate pressure and a lifting, the delicate pressure coming from the first finger versus thumb and second, the pressure sometimes involving the third finger as well, and the lifting involving the fourth finger and releasing simultaneously the pressure on the first, so that the bow lifts off the string easily with no work of the fourth against the first. Sometimes the lifting is aided by the third finger, sometimes even by the second. All these different combinations involve on one stroke slight pressure and lift, then on the return stroke slight pressure and lift; and sometimes in the opposite way the stroke can be lifted first and then pressed at the end of the stroke. Each combination should be practised. This will evolve a very fine subtlety of reaction in the right hand. The 'pressure' should always be associated with a spreading of the fingers, the fingers involved in the pressure, that is one and three, one and two. During the moment when the bow is lifted off the string the actual hand should be completely relaxed and slightly hanging from the wrist with the fourth finger more or less elongated by its very resting on the stick. That almost alone should be sufficient to lift it against the pivot of the thumb and the second and third fingers which prevent the bow from falling out of the hand. In fact in pianissimo strokes the first finger and the thumb, and even the second and third, are only there to guide the bow not to exert any pressure.

The delicate hold or grip of the right hand on the bow can be introduced – in the course of one uninterrupted stroke – once, twice, three times or more. It is the precursor to the portato. This is a stroke which brings a gentle emphasis to each note, and, by applying it very gradually over a whole stroke, it will cause a crescendo. Conversely, a diminuendo is caused by releasing it. But the release must occur together with a lightening of the weight, just as the increasing tension must occur with an increase of allowable weight, and eventually pressure, as the stick stiffens, and is allowed to take the maximum pressure that is indeed required in the upper half of the bow, to achieve a big sound there.

The reason why so few violinists can make a crescendo as they draw the bow towards the tip is that they have not mastered this spread of pressure brought to bear along the length of the bow by the fingers and the stiffening of the stick. It should therefore always be remembered that pressure does not come only from the first finger on the bow digging the stick into the string. It comes from the *spreading* of that pressure, a pressure brought to bear along the whole arch of the fingers of the right hand through the knuckles and against the thumb. Sometimes this pressure can be brought to bear by two fingers only.

I must emphasize that when we speak of bow pressure on the string, we only mean that the bow is pulling or pushing the string – pulling in a down-bow or pushing in an up-bow – and by means of the string is pushing or pulling the violin, and the reaction must be felt throughout both hands and shoulders. Pressure as such must not be interpreted simply as vertical pressure. This would only crush the string and prevent it from vibrating. The object of the bow drawn over the string is to pull the string away from its middle immobile position, at the same time allowing it to return and undulate, vibrate between positions on either side of the middle. If it is pressed down vertically you simply crush the sound. The object of pulling the string is to give it the widest possible amplitude of vibration.

It is a good exercise to imagine that the up-bow stroke begins in the first quarter of the bow with only the first finger on the bow, the second quarter with the second, the third with the third, and finally the fourth quarter with the fourth finger on the stroke; while all the time the fingers have also been together, with the forearm rotating clockwise, the fingers pushing the bow into the up-bow and ending at the frog, all four fingers on the bow and the fingers in an extended up-bow position, wrist depressed. This can be practised most easily when moving from the G string at the tip to the E string at the frog over the four strings. Conversely a down-bow would move from the E string down to the G string, ending with only the first finger on the bow in a falling elongated position.

It is then a good idea to try the opposite – the same thing happening in the fingers and bow, but beginning the up-bow stroke on the E string and ending with all four fingers on the G string. This is extremely useful, and is in fact the basic exercise which prepares for the two different rotational directions which we have already mentioned (see p. 45). Practise a down-bow on a lower string to an up-bow on an upper string, then, conversely, a down-bow on an upper string to an up-bow on a lower string.

For exercises over the four strings it is good to put the hand in the most exacting position, which is first finger on the E string and fourth finger on the G string.

String crossings and bounce exercises

It is very important to master the two different rotational directions from one string to another. This should be done first between strings, then between two strings with one in between, and finally between the two extreme strings, thus gradually mastering the full range of the arc. It will be noticed that in doing the anti-clockwise rotation – that is, down-bow on the E string and up-bow on the G – the down-bow coincides with the motion into the depressed wrist and therefore the arm describes a greater arc, the forearm going lower on the E and higher on the G than in the opposite clockwise rotation, where the hand and finger positions reach the G string without the arm having to be raised to the full height of the G string. Thus the motion through the clockwise direction – that is when the bow plays down-bow on the G string and up-bow on the E string – is achieved with the aid of the wrist and the fingers, the arm moving in the smaller circle, whereas in the anti-clockwise direction it is the arm that is moving in a larger circle and the wrist and fingers in the smaller.

To feel the flexibility and balance, as it were, of the bow, it should be held in our second stage of balance (see p. 23), achieved without effort but simply by the weight of the second, third and fourth fingers resting on the bow and balancing its length over the pivot of the thumb; then let the bow drop on to the string by releasing the fourth and third fingers. The bow will fall on the string and bounce up again. This should be practised until it is possible to allow the bow to bounce three or four, or five, or six, or more, times in the course of a short or a long stroke at different speeds – different speeds in stroke, different speeds in balance – both on down- and up-bows, and on all strings, and moving from lower strings to upper strings and *vice versa*. This develops a very sensitive and delicate and balanced hold in the hand, a hold that is never so tight that the bow cannot fall and bounce, and yet never so loose that the bow is dropped, or control of the motion of the bow is lost. The fingers should also apply their grip to down-bow motion, and *vice versa*.

When the bounce has been mastered the string crossings should be done in all parts of the bow, with one bounce note to each stroke and the bow leaving the string at the end of each stroke. The strokes can be very short, as in a very light bounce, or they can be long and yet separated by the bow lifted off the string. They can eventually be\done in martelé and indeed in every form of attack from the sudden martelé to the most gentle landing with no suddenness on impact.

These exercises will give the violinist a tremendous control over every kind of sound and attack. They can be done in conjunction with left hand jumps or slides, double stops: anything should be combined.

The range of violin bowing

Among the most miraculous qualities of violin-bowing are the complete range of:

1. *Attack* – from the gentlest to the decisive and finally even the brutal.
2. *Length of stroke* – from the shortest to the longest, the fastest to the slowest.
3. *Legato* – in infinite melodic extension, eternally, as if drawing on God's breath.
4. *Inflection* – from all types of accent to faster or slower variations in volume and inflection.

These modes of expression depend on the relationships of speeds, weights and trajectories of motion between shoulder-blades, shoulders, upper and lower arms, hands, each and all the fingers, and all joints – elbows, wrists and joints of thumb and fingers – in terms of the awareness of the sensations of floating or carrying, of the hold, or of pressure in varying degrees of active and passive.

Thus, for example, steep, sudden attack demands an immediate departure, already at speed, with the bow exercising enough pressure on the string (only just enough) to pull the string away (in the direction of the stroke) from its straight line, independently of any sound. To achieve this, a slight pressure of the forefinger (and co-operation of balancing fingers) is required to keep the bow on one spot for a split second, whilst limb and fingers softly obey the general direction of the stroke (down-bow or up-bow), gathering speed until the moment when the fingers (knuckles) – having reached almost the extreme depressed position (down-bow) or opposite (up-bow) – yank (delicately) the bow at their speed. To accentuate the accent even more, the fingers can yield to a voluntary throw, overtaking the average (as it were) limb speed of the stroke, thus obeying the principle of anticipating a motion with the stressing of its opposite (just before a down-bow, the up-bow should take on increased dash, speed and lightness; and vice versa).

The floating sensation of limb is essential for legato. For a change of bow at the frog, weight and pressure between limb, fingers, bow, bowhair, string, bridge and left-hand thumb and fingers must give way to a momentarily recaptured floating feeling. Let the bow hang from your fingers, your thumb soft, flexible and pliable at its base and its joints, despite the minimal hold which is between thumb and second (and other) fingers.

The stringed instruments and wind (except for electronically assisted keyboards) are the only ones which, like the voice, can play a true legato which allows a note both to increase in volume, leading into the next, or to decrease. Plucked, percussion or keyboard instruments cannot achieve this. They must rely upon clusters of notes which consecutively (as with film cameras) or simultaneously (harmony) bind or relate the notes of the melodic sequences. By playing successive notes softer, a legato feeling can be created. The pianist or the guitarist must be something of a magician in that he gives the illusion of melodic continuity, despite the inevitable diminuendo following the initial impact of any given note.

The thumb motion can be conceived in four sections, two down-bows and two up-bows.
1. Down-bow. Thumb moves from the folded position to the elongated base position thus providing the motive origin.
2. Up-bow. Thumb back to original folded (1) position.
3. Continuation of a new up-bow. Thumb continues in up direction with first joint unfolding.
4. Return to (1) position on down-bow as described.

These motions (with the co-operation of the other fingers) apply to the finger motion alone. As soon as the whole-limb stroke is engaged, the opposite strokes result. Thus (1) becomes an up-bow, with wrist pulling, etc. (much longer than original (1)). (2) remains an up-bow, etc. (3) is a down-bow. (4) is a down-bow, hand and fingers maintaining momentum. There is again every degree of proportion in terms of relative speed, weight, pressure and distance between these above sets of examples.

Therefore each day's work must cover the basics, i.e. the establishing of extremes and averages in all categories: pp, mf, ff, very slow, medium, fast, etc. The natural action of expressive playing will fill in the degrees. But without establishing the span or range (always beginning from 'zero' – zero distance, zero pressure, zero speed, etc. – and co-ordinating whole body motion) the infinitely varied and subtle expressions of living communication will never take place – or only inadequately.

Some specific strokes*

Martelé. The beginnings of martelé should always start piano and not forte. The attack should simply be the minimum grip of the bow on the string. The pull should consist first of the 'beginning' of the stroke. By the beginning I mean the drawing position of the wrist and arm, for no stroke should start unless it has something – even if only vestigial remains – of drawing the tone at the beginning of the stroke. And in the martelé that is immediately followed by the throwing motion of the arm. These two motions – drawing and throwing – account for all the different strokes and vary, of course, in their proportion, their length, their time duration, and their speed. The same applies to the up-bow. The bow should be on the string and the stroke begun with just the minimum amount of pressure required to pull the string away from its straight, taut position. Thus the sound begins with the martelé suddenness.

* see also glossary.

Later the timing can be so perfected that the arm and hand and bow can fall on to the string from a height, and lightly pull the string with this martelé grip, and catch one, two, three or four strings simultaneously, in fortissimo, but without any scratch, elegantly and cleanly. The violinist must for ever bear in mind the purity of sound which is his continuous aim.

Staccato. Staccato is a series of martelés on one stroke, a throw of the fingers in the direction of the stroke repeatedly; but in fast staccato it is really vibratory response in the fingers, while holding the bow in a balanced hold, and drawing in such a way that the bow vibrates on the string in the direction of the stroke. It is a continuous stroke and the violinist is no longer aware of a separating process. He thinks rather of four, or six, or eight, or whatever number of notes, at a time.

In a down-bow staccato, beginning at the extreme frog, the bow is in the extreme up-bow position – that is wrist depressed, fingers elongated into the up-bow pointing towards the tip. The opposite hold applies in an up-bow staccato. The staccato should be practised with the arm and fingers both pulling the bow and throwing or pushing the bow, in both down- and up-bows. This develops a great latitude and freedom of motion. It is important to combine the up- and down-bows, after having done them separately, with a change of direction at every point, including the extremes.

The student's first strokes should no doubt be equal détachés in the middle of the bow, not using more than a few inches. These should gradually be lengthened on both sides until eventually the whole bow is used. A further stage is the rhythm of crotchet, two quavers, crotchet, two quavers, whole bow, two half-bows, whole up-bow, two half-bows, whole down-bow, two half-bows, whole up-bow, two half-bows. This allows the bow to keep moving at the same speed while varying the rhythm merely by the length of the bow stroke used.

Gradually this can be transformed into using the whole bow on the one stroke, and then only a quarter, or an eighth, or a sixteenth of the bow, the notes becoming correspondingly faster and the rhythm beginning to achieve a dotted effect.

Then the middle stroke can be left out, achieving a completely dotted rhythm effect; and finally only the dotted rhythm – the long note having been shortened. The main time is then taken up by a rest, so that a very short dotted rhythm is achieved, at all parts of the bow and in all types of string crossings, even at the frog, from G to the E string, and from E down to the G in an instant – a lightning reflex.

The up-bow 'brake' is released by 'giving' in your knuckles, fingers and wrist. By making *short* arm up-bow strokes, your hand will *follow through* to regain a new, identical 'brakes' starting point.

The same applies, reversed, for the down-bow stroke.

Portato. This is a softer version of the staccato exercise, with particular attention to the follow-motion of the thumb.

The up-bow portato pressure derives from (a) your first finger *down* and *out*, and *up* towards the point, and (b) your third finger *in* with your thumb rolling the stick *against* the outward first finger push. The whole must be co-ordinated with soft, easy, flowing staccato motion, your hand eager to regain, *with* your thumb, its follow-through, forward up-bow position.

The portato down-bow requires the same type of pressure, but occurring on the lean of down-knuckles and not on the up-knuckles pull.

The change of bow occurs easily on half of the full motion, as explained in the above staccato exercise.

Being in a sense a smooth form of staccato, the bow does not stop for each note, but makes a separate inflexion on each note and applies an added pressure on each note.

Again, this is a formation of the fingers, flexibly arriving at approximate pressure positions, but never going to extreme positions, as in early staccato exercises. Inflexion occurs on the way to and before arriving at the staccato pressure position and is, in fact, immediately released. It is a smooth, easy stroke which enhances the moulding of a phrase and develops a great gamut of tone volume and colour.

Flying staccato actually comes most easily. It is important for the bow to be perfectly balanced in a very soft hold with hardly any pressure on the string. The initial motion is a lateral motion of the wrist to the right, but again very small, corresponding to a fraction of the distance travelled by the bow on any one single note.

In the up-bow retake, as in the Mendelssohn Concerto, the elbow-push occurs simultaneously with a falling hand from the wrist. It is definitely not a lifting of the bow off the strings with the hand.

The staccato and portato exercises should be correlated with chromatic scales on single strings or on two strings (double stops) in the left hand. This is an important co-ordination, for it brings into play in rhythmic connection both arms and shoulders. This must be practised combining the up-bow with both ascending and descending scales and vice-versa.

Vibrato. Vibrato, which is the hallmark of the violinist's tone, is a natural result of the exercises and motions I have tried to describe. The same motion is at the basis of the vibrato, a change of position, and even of the finger fall.

It is good to practise the change of position between, say, the second finger in a lower position and the first finger in a higher position, or the fourth in a lower and the first in a higher, or the third in a lower and the second in a higher – in other words, giving the wrist that maximum flick which spells eventual speed and accuracy. Practise also in double stops between the third and fourth fingers, playing the interval of the fourth in a lower position, and first and second fingers, playing the interval of the fourth in a higher position. The same exercise can be applied to the third, etc.

Finger fall, which is the basic motion of the fingers as in

scales, in vibrato or in the oscillation of the finger on the string, is, in fact, composed of fingers, knuckles, wrist and arm oscillation; there is no part which should be rigid or excluded. The oscillations should be practised in a measured way with finger fall. Thus the oscillation which leads to the higher sound is timed with the finger fall of an upper finger. Thus the second finger falls while the first is oscillating, and falls on to the string at the moment the oscillation reaches the higher pitch. All this should automatically be practised the opposite way as well, the upper finger falling when the oscillation reaches its lower extreme. In this way, again, flexibility is enhanced and the readiness to meet any situation is increased.

As a typical exercise, hold the D on the A string between the thumb and second finger; then try to pull the violin away from the hold of the chin and collar-bone, and allow the wrist to bend out; then, while maintaining this pull, exercise the finger and thumb in such a way as to bring the hand back to the original position. You are doing what are known as resistance exercises, strengthening the inner muscles of the finger and the thumb. Now push the violin into the neck and go into a depressed wrist and depressed knuckle position; then while maintaining this pressure, push the knuckles and the wrist out. You are developing a different set of muscles.

Each muscle must be developed separately, so that there will never be a confusion; two sets of muscles must not be used at the same time. This is the basis of the seizure, the confusion, the frustration, the terrible blight of violin playing.

Vibrato must be as varied as the weather of England, and always beautiful and sweet. It can be very narrow and fast, producing a gleaming, penetrating sound – as wonderful in pianissimo as in fortissimo; pure, with so little vibration as to be almost a choir-boy sound, or so much as to be like a brilliant light, so intense is its penetrating effect. It can be slow and wide, it can be fast and wide, it can be velvety, it can be burning with passion. It can be all of these, but these powers are only developed by exercises such as those I have described, which engage the whole range, and every degree of range, of strength and flexibility and sensitivity of all the joints and muscles involved. And a great amount of concentration is essential. Playing and practising the violin demand work of the mind.

Developing a good bow arm

The following exercises for martelé and staccato are invaluable for developing a good bow-arm.*

Martelé and staccato require a lateral movement in the wrist. This is a very small one, but it is nonetheless crucial to speed and accuracy. In the release of a down-bow, look for this slight lateral motion to the left; and in the release of an up-bow, observe it happening to the right.

It is important to distinguish between the grip of the bow on the string – during which moment the bow is tugging (pulling) at the string, but is immobile in that it is not moving in relation to the string – and the ensuing stroke itself – which must be very light and fast.

Starting at the frog, make a *finger* down-bow sufficient to raise your wrist into a high (up-bow) position, moving your hand slightly and laterally to the right at the wrist, sufficient to pull the string slightly without drawing any sound and short of scratching in the down-bow direction.

Retaining the pull, release the pressure by allowing your fingers to assume a low (down-bow) position and the bow will glide over the string quickly, smoothly and without bounce. This is the whole-bow martelé stroke.

For the up-bow martelé stroke, make a finger up-bow, pushing your hand into a low down-bow position and moving your hand laterally to the left at the wrist, and with your whole arm pushing in the up-bow direction. This up-bow pressure should be felt all the way back into your shoulder,

*I owe much of the inspiration for this exposition to the Assistant to the great Professor Yankileavitch, Mr Andreevsky, who expounded on staccato to the children at my school.

which should be felt to be pulled out away from your neck. Release the pressure by allowing your fingers to extend and your wrist to rise into the up-bow position, the lateral motion going into the right, which will result in the bow moving smoothly and lightly towards the frog.

The next exercise is, of course, two notes in one stroke, half a bow-length to each. You stop the bow and grip the string by making the fingers assume the initial position of stroke. It is important to keep a *constant* pull (or push) on down-bow or up-bow. Pull with the arm, so that in fact *only* the altered finger position stops the stroke, and, by the same token, allows it to resume its course. Then do this with three notes, then four notes, until you may do eight, ten, twelve or more notes to one bow-stroke.

Spend a week, a month, or as long as necessary to master the first stage. Never hurry or become impatient. Spend as much time as necessary on each of the following stages, accelerating the metronome by one number (say 100 to 101 or 102) every few days.

When playing continuous alternate down-bows and up-bows, the last position on the down-bow should be the beginning of the up-bow and vice versa. In other words, whether you are playing one note or ten notes, when you arrive at the end of your stroke on the last note, the hand should not return to the position required for each renewed down-bow of the stroke (i.e. the high position) but should simply do half the motion and remain in the low position, with the arm immediately pushing in the up-bow direction. This is the beginning of the up-bow. This exercise ensures a very good bow change of direction, because the direction is automatically assumed at the end of the last stroke even before the new direction begins.

A further stage is to play two notes very quickly on one impulse, on very little bow. Repeat such pairs of notes along the whole length of the bow, six, seven, eight and more pairs. It will be noticed that the first note of each pair on a down-bow occurs when the hand releases its high position, allowing the bow to travel *slightly*; and the second note occurs when the hand resumes its original position, pushing the bow along. The pair of notes thus represents a rapid pull-push. The opposite occurs on the up-bow.

This is a very important exercise and stage in staccato playing, as it relieves the arm, and even the hand, from being responsible for each note. The one impulse can later be allowed to include in rapid succession three notes, then four in little sudden fast groups of notes, beginning with the repeated notes. Still later, look for that part of the bow which lends itself to the easiest and most rapid staccato – the upper part – but try to extend this control as near to the frog as you can comfortably get.

Retakes

The last movement of the Mendelssohn Concerto is an example of up-bow retake strokes. The motion consists of various parts which happen almost simultaneously:

1. A short upper arm up-bow stroke.
2. An elbow push, which is also a fall toward the side of the body, simultaneous with
3. A falling hand at a rising wrist.
4. A softness in the two fingers allowing the bow to fall on to the string in a tilting position that is a point lower than the frog.
5. It is the reciprocal resilience of the string and the bow which causes the bounce, *not* any lifting from finger or wrist. The very first stroke may require to be lifted with the third finger on the stick, but all the subsequent ones no longer need lifting. It is sufficient to keep the first and second fingers on the bow fairly closely without the third and fourth on the stick. The only effort required is, with the help of your elbow and your falling hand, to accelerate the bow's natural fall on to the string, thus ensuring the bounce.

In retakes, not only does the elbow fall considerably closer

78

Plate 4. Rotating the violin between thumb and fingers
Plate 5. Rotating the violin anti-clockwise (as seen by the playing violinist)

↓ 5

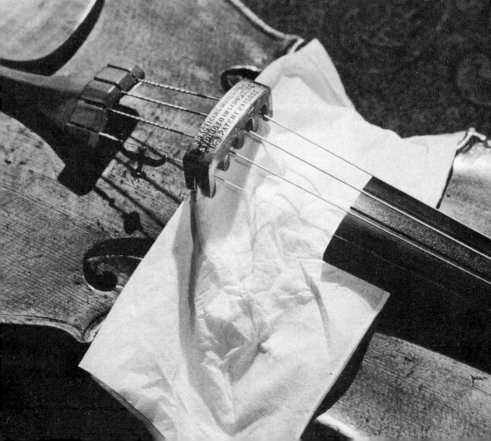

to the side of the body, as described below, but it moves again on each retake *perceptibly* forward.

In retakes, the right elbow comes closer to the body side, repeating this closing motion on each retake. It is, of course, closer to the body on the E string than on lower strings. This proximity to the side of the body (or in other words this lowering of the elbow) is necessary in order to pick the bow vertically as the hand drops. This is concurrent with slight rotation of the bow stick towards the flatter-haired position.

Ricochet

Ricochet down-bow is produced by letting the hand fall from the wrist from an initially raised position; it is, in fact, a wave motion. The bow must be held so lightly that the smallest, shortest fall will cause the bow to bounce off the string. The hold is so delicate as to allow the fourth finger visibly to bend *passively* with each bow bounce.

Practise the up-bow, too, and continuous down- and up-bows to four, three and two notes (bounced) to each stroke in different parts of the bow.

In ricochet, the preparatory lifting of the hand is in reality one and the same motion as the depression of the wrist which is part of the initial détaché pull, which in the case of ricochet takes place in the air. Every ricochet stroke begins with a small détaché pull (down- and up-bows), not big enough to alter the balance of four fingers on the stick.

For a soft delicate effect, carry the bow above but very near the string and allow it to bounce in delicate balanced bow-hand and occupying stroke.

Spiccato

Play spiccato very softly. It should be fast and smooth, varied with very small strokes. Keep your finger joints and thumb joints soft. Use a large component of détaché, i.e. pull motion, not throw action (as described). Always keep the bow on the string, *never* lifted.

Plate 6. Thumb mobility

Plate 7. The least irritating form for practising – it spares the ears of both player and neighbours, while the tissue keeps the violin varnish free of resin

Five
Practising

Discipline

Many violinists start out with the idea of becoming solo performers. This is entirely wrong. In fact students at my school have as much experience in chamber music and orchestral playing as they do in solo work, and it is no demotion to become a chamber music player or an orchestral musician, let alone a concert master or leader. But in each case an earnest and serious approach is important, and whether the student practises one hour a day or ten hours a day, depending on his ambition and his stamina, his physique and his way of practising, it must be done with the same care, the same exacting attention and precision; and even if he is a child, who can only practise ten minutes, it is important that these ten minutes be spent to the full value.

Practice must be looked upon as a joy and a privilege, not as a sentence. Too many young violinists with ambitious parents have been sentenced to work. Obviously it is important for the teacher and the parent to instill the proper attitude of discipline and seriousness. If a child has decided to become a violinist and has chosen that vocation, then his training must be given its full importance and everything done so that the child advances as quickly and as solidly as possible. No one should say: 'Oh well, today you don't have to work if you don't feel like it', or 'Let's have a picnic', or 'Let's do something else'. Once the child has chosen the violin and has lessons, his training must be respected and the same period of the day each day must be given to work. It is of the utmost importance from the very beginning to develop the proper attitude, the proper sensitivity and reverence for the instrument, for the profession, and for the future.

The student himself should strive to be calm, precise, concentrated and purposeful. Determination does not come in sudden spurts of earth-shaking ferocity; it is measured rather by the capacity to maintain effort quietly over a long haul. Determination is quiet, unyielding, yet patient and relaxed practice, for four or five hours a day, six days a week, year in, year out with holidays of a week or so every few months.

Developing stamina

No student, I believe, should tolerate from himself any awkwardness or ugly sound or impatience. It is better to put the violin down when tired and fed up, and to take a few breaths of fresh air. But at the same time it is important always to go a little bit beyond your capacity. The element of over-strain, provided it is quickly dissipated in proper stretching and breathing exercises, the element of over-exertion, provided it doesn't create a bad habit of playing with unbalance and stress, teach us to expect of ourselves more than we can give. To develop strength, stamina and resilience you must always go slightly beyond the point of initial fatigue – but not too far, just a little.

I remember my last lesson with Enesco in Sinia, in the heart of the Carpathian Alps, on a late autumn day with thunder and lightning wrapping the snow-covered peaks of the mountains and the last colours of autumn fading from the wonderful deciduous forests. He was teaching me the *Chaconne*. I played it through once and he seemed to approve, but he made me play it through a second time, and then a third time. I was eleven years old and the *Chaconne* is a tremendous piece requiring great reserves of every kind. I shall never forget that lesson and he did it to good purpose.

81

Part One: The Violin
The need for relaxation

We must never forget how much we learn, assimilate, absorb during sleep and rest. It is between bouts of effort that the great part of achievement takes place, during the interruptions for rethinking, for resting, for restoring the circulation. One effort will not achieve anything, but repeated efforts with rests in between, with or without sleep, will achieve a great deal. Concentration of thought leaves its residue in the subconscious.

I sometimes take a violin along on holiday and work gently on small technical things, for the mind is better able to concentrate on such details when it is not concerned with the concert the next day.

Using a mute

The advantages of using a mute are twofold. That it is kinder to your neighbour is obvious: you have only to try practising at night in an hotel without a mute to discover that the space controlled by a violinist impinges on other people's space. The revolt is rapid: ringing telephone, protests, bangs on the wall. Once in a while they have heard of the violinist and may feel slightly ashamed.

Once, before I had learned the advantages of practising with a mute, I was travelling from New York to Washington on the morning train and I had to practise because I was giving a concert that very afternoon. I had what is known as a day drawing-room, which is a separate private room at the end of the long open Pullman carriage. Gradually there was a mounting revolt among the passengers and one by one they came and banged at the locked door. It was a five-hour trip and I had to work. I continued, notwithstanding. But I realized that I had to do something to save myself from being lynched as soon as I opened the door before disembarking. I struck upon the good idea of playing Schubert's *Ave Maria* thus touching a communal sentiment of prayer and reverence. I played with all my heart with a wonderfully rich vibrato – and I knew that after that I could emerge forgiven and safe.

But the use of a mute is also kinder to the violinist: for with it he can concentrate better on the physical sensations of playing and on the quality of sound he produces than he can when assailed with the full blast of his own sound directly under his ear.

The doctor usually practises together with his team. The business man, too, and the factory worker exercise their profession away from home, reserving their hearth for conjugal responsibilities, for relaxation and for family. But the musician brings his very personal preoccupations *into* the home and, however soothing music may sometimes be, practice is more often either dull or simply noisily irritating. Here is yet another reason why I earnestly recommend practising with a mute.

Moreover the violinist's burden is not limited to office hours; he carries it around with him all day and all night. In fact, he must learn to *clear* his mind for normal life and live with wife and family for at least part of the day, and to do this he must discipline his mind and work so that he may achieve the greatest results with the least time. Even so, his poor wife (or her poor husband) will have to bear many burdens in a taxing and selfless supporting role.

Variety in practice

Remember that the violin can be played standing, sitting or squatting. I have spent countless hours travelling by train in my compartment, squatting on the bed, practising. The Indian violinist plays his instrument, in his own classical style, squatting. The chamber music player and the orchestra player are seated; and the soloist plays standing. Standing is of course the position which achieves the greatest swing and attack, and in which the violinist commands his audience to the fullest extent of his power.

Every violinist should practise in all three positions – standing, seated and sometimes squatting.

Practising on a viola. One of the best habits a violinist can make is to practise his whole violin repertoire on a viola with a viola bow*, as distances, pressures and weights are greater and a reserve of flexibility and strength is built up. There is *absolutely* no danger of playing out of tune; on the contrary, the ear learns to direct and adjust the fingers, as they become stronger, more sensitive, more flexible and faster in response to practice trills and ordinary finger falls.

Thought and analysis

Even when the student is not practising with his violin he must devote some time to thinking about music; to studying scores and to going through his music in his mind without violin *or* score.

The image of a particular work is projected in various aspects. There is the physiological, physical sensation associated with playing; the digital memory; the visualization of the page where the note occurs in the score; the intellectual knowledge of the structure of a piece or of a movement; the emotional guide to the effective sequence.

Continuity is all-important. After thorough analysis, the violinist must go quietly through the work, either in his mind's eye, or with the fingers with a mute on, pianissimo, observing every smallest sensation but allowing the work to flow on to its natural end.

Finally let me emphasize that the violinist should never practise in a dead or automatic way until he knows that everything is happening correctly, even when he forgets about it. Your commands, the commands to your limbs, to your nerves and muscles, should gradually be taken over by

*As few violinists are lucky enough to own a viola as well, this may necessitate borrowing.

an ever-retreating consciousness, leaving you ever freer and freer, so that you may commune with the music, and your technique may become the automatic reflex of your emotional, spiritual and intellectual impulses.

Six
The Violinist in Action

The leader

The concert master, the leader, the first violinist in an orchestra, holds a unique position in the violinist's world. He requires all the qualities of supreme musicianship, outstanding technique and the ability to sight-read. He must be proficient in playing alone, for there are hair-raising solo passages for the first violinist in many orchestral works. But these qualities are not enough, and there are many solo violinists and chamber music players who could not fit automatically into the position of orchestral leader. For the leader must have the qualities of leadership and also of submission to authority.

On the one hand he is very much the leader, both of his section and of the orchestra. He is responsible for his section, for the second violins, and indeed for the whole string section. He must suggest ideal phrasing, find the right bowings and fingerings, monitor the sections and see that they all play well and in tune. He is also responsible for the tuning of all instruments and for the discipline of all the players in the orchestra, and they in their turn must give of their best, and respect his knowledge, and the discipline of performance and work he exacts.

But he, by the same token, is subservient to and must respect the conductor, accepting that position as ultimate arbiter, as prime mover above his own position. So he must be equally skilled in serving as in leading, equally at ease as a soloist as when playing as one of the section. He must submit to the discipline of the group and maintain the inspiration and freedom of a soloist. While playing in unison with his group he cannot allow himself to do anything erratic. He must play as planned, with the same bowings and fingerings and inflections; but at the same time he must be ready to follow the inspiration of a conductor who may each moment be alive to unexpected inflections, to a fresh discovery. (And the conductor too, of course, must know to what practical extent this impulse can be conveyed through the leader and to what extent it must be modified if the orchestra is unprepared for his sudden vision.)

A great leader will understand what the conductor wishes and what he is about. He will be able to communicate to the orchestra the impulse and the living flow of the conductor's conception. Of course it is during rehearsals that the most important work is done and it is then that the conductor must be sure to touch upon every detail which will come into play later, so that the orchestra is well aware and prepared for whatever he may wish to do at performance.

All this requires a very flexible, a very subtle, a very sensitive character. To shift easily between authority and obedience, whilst remaining the self-same person at heart, is one of the most civilized of refinements. In the case of the leader it is the passing on of the illumination, the search for more expressive and perfect performances which is perhaps his major role. He is one link – a very essential link – in the chain between conception and inspiration and their realization. This chain links composer first, then conductor, then leader, and finally the musicians of the orchestra without whom no conception would be of any use.

The leader of the second violins

There is yet another very special career for the violinist and that is as second violin, whether in a quartet or as leader of the second violins in an orchestra. He relates to the first violin in much the same way that the first violin relates to the conductor.

Given the voice of the second violin he has to play, he must possess certain very distinct qualities, for the particular characteristics of the second violin part are such that he does not come to play the shiny melodies, the leading voice, as often as the first. Very often he must play the typical second violin accompaniments which are tremendously demanding in terms of rhythmic security, polish, deftness, sharpness of delineation, shortness and precision of notes, length of notes, variance of notes. These in his case are far more exacting than the first violinist's in the sense that they demand a totally dedicated ear, total self-discipline, and no – or very little – opportunity of expansion or self-expression. Unlike the melodic line which has a wider margin of personal involvement, of personal commentary, of personal style, the second violin has no opportunity for this self-indulgence and must observe the strictest control of his own impulses and a total subservience to the need of the line above him and in fact of all the other instruments of the orchestra. His playing of what we call the inner part of the harmonies is a most precise task and I have the greatest respect for it; and I have known violinists who were ideal leaders of the second violin section, so good at it that one could almost say that that was what they were born for.

The orchestral player

But in speaking of the orchestra we must not forget those who play behind the leader, those who sit in the back chairs, for they too are essential. It is terribly important for the conductor and the leader to maintain the morale of the back chairs, for when all is said and done an orchestra is not a matter of a few individuals, but a body of musicians who are giving themselves and their souls to the music they are playing, and unless this inspiration permeates every last chair the orchestra is carrying a burden of dead wood.

The orchestral musician in the string sections who does not play in the first chairs has much to be grateful for if his temperament is suited to his job. He doesn't carry the responsibility of initiative, but that of collaboration, and he enjoys the companionship which is denied those who shoulder their responsibilities alone. He may also have more free time – to play chamber music, to teach, and to indulge in many other activities and hobbies. It is not unrewarding to be a last chair in a good orchestra under a good conductor. It can be a very happy life, but the violinist must understand what it is all about and be temperamentally suited to his position.

The chamber musician

The conductor will do well to encourage the orchestra to use its free time, in fact to make time, to form into various groups – chamber orchestras, sextets, octets, wind ensembles – wherein each player can keep up the standard of his own musicianship and performance. For this purpose there is nothing as good as chamber music. We shall always come back to chamber music – the quartet, the string quartet in particular – as the highest form of musical activity, as the most perfect blending, the most exquisite adjustment, giving the purest musical satisfaction to those who play and to those who listen. It is not aimed to produce mammoth effects in volume on mammoth audiences in mammoth halls. It is the expression of a cultivated society, of cultivated minds and refined spirits in human beings. It is perhaps the greatest contribution Europe has made to civilization.

Chamber music should be played, almost, by amateurs rather than by professionals. Naturally the professional string quartet is an amazing achievement, but the civilization that I would love to know rests on amateur performance, on those innumerable small groups that gather in private homes – too few today, the age of 'The Knob'. These groups gather on certain evenings, perhaps once a week, to play chamber music. It is my prayer and hope that, with the renewed interest in music, with the better teaching of music in schools, with the yearly advance in the quality of teachers and students, my dream will come true: that, when the present generation grow up, they will have the means to play for themselves, for their friends, for their families, to make chamber music at home; and that composers will reward them with contemporary compositions which they will enjoy as much as they will always enjoy the musical heritage of the past.

On being a soloist*

There is a life-enhancing sense of exhilaration when playing the solo part of a concerto with orchestra. To be the one voice among the many, to be carried by their support, to be challenged by their comment, to be inspired by a body of sound of infinite variety and to be entrusted with the leading statement – these are indeed heady sensations which only conquerors know. Yet, unlike Genghis Khan, and fortunately both for himself and his followers, the soloist is both servant and defendant, submitting continually to the judgement of his fellow-musicians both among his public and among his critics.

This is a very good thing, and is a measure of the evolution between our Genghis Khan and a high civil servant, a prime minister or a president, for instance. In my experience, there is nothing nearer human infallibility in its musical and human judgement than the collective opinion of an orchestra. It reflects the same good sense and higher instinct as does the collective voice of an experienced electorate. Collective opinion must, of course, neglect doubts, anxieties, lack of trust and many currents of thought. Yet the minority is as important as the majority in shaping the *total* verdict and it is, of course, for the most part nonsense to speak of a unanimous mandate or of an unqualified victory. The reader must forgive this digression, but by now he should be accustomed to my crab-wise mind and its constant preoccupation to relate the singular to the collective, the unique to the universal.

To return to the soloist. Aware, as he must be, of the other musicians, his immediate concern is to be at one with the conductor. Under ideal chamber music conditions, when a

*Here the reader must forgive me if I write about my own experience.

group of colleagues is closely identified with the soloist and when it has a sensitive and competent leader, it is possible to experience supreme and electric contact between players without having to make a detour via the intermediary, the conductor. I enjoy this relationship with the Menuhin Festival Orchestra and Robert Masters. But generally this is only possible with works originally conceived to be played in this style, i.e. without conductor, the soloist and first violinist (the leader) leading, or with works small enough in their orchestration to allow every member of the group to listen and adjust. For larger works this form of performance would require so much rehearsal as to be impracticable, although I have often played, for example, the Beethoven concerto and the Viotti A Minor with my group. On the other hand – despite the heightened awareness of each player and the genuine satisfaction every instrumentalist derives from the responsibility, the trust, the importance and independence accorded him in playing without a conductor (he is generally happy to be able to make music instead of following a beat!) – when a great or even just a good conductor comes along it is deeply rewarding to engage in a dialogue.

The dialogue between conductor and soloist must be played out with courtesy on both sides, the soloist giving fair warning, playing freely, yes, but never erratically, his phrasing appearing logical and inevitable, his breathing so natural that music and musicians alike fall into place. A gifted conductor contributes interpretative insight – that magic which is almost hypnotic – and a quality of inspiration which makes everyone, including the soloist, play more beautifully than they thought possible.

The etiquette of a soloist is extremely important. It is definitely out of place for him or her to suggest anything to the orchestra directly – only to the conductor. The conductor may then specifically ask the soloist to demonstrate a bowing, fingering or phrasing, which the soloist may have mentioned or suggested to the conductor. The soloist must follow the conductor in entrances or final ritardandos. Similarly, he must follow the conductor wherever he is sharing a passage with another orchestral player or players and wherever both depend upon the conductor. Whichever party – soloist or orchestra – has more notes to the beat determines the tempo. If interpretations differ too widely or are incompatible, the soloist must explain quietly and very clearly the correction he would appreciate. He must always listen to orchestral truths with great attention. The part the orchestra plays is of course an integral part of any work, and as far as possible the conductor's and the soloist's interpretation should match in tempo and in phrasing. It is quite allowable to turn slightly towards the orchestra to listen better and the soloist should never try to distract the audience from conductor or orchestra. When playing the solo part, however, the violinist (except when sharing the podium with other soloists, as in double concerti, etc.) should face the audience squarely. Of course wherever necessary the violinist must take note of the beat and at crucial moments he must look at the conductor, but only out of the corner of his eye.

Some conductors are better accompanists than others. Bruno Walter and John Barbirolli, for example, were superlatively good. Alas, they are among those already gone. Toscanini, on the other hand, was no accompanist at all, despite the fact that he was supreme in Italian opera. Growing up in an Italian opera pit, he should have been outstanding as an accompanist, and no doubt could have been, had he been temperamentally suited, but he was strongly possessed by his own interpretation and could not conceive of any other! It was nonetheless a great thrill to play with him, for whatever he did was genial, even if others who tried to imitate him inevitably came to grief. I am happy to say that among the younger generation there are brilliant conductors, Zubin Mehta and Gary Bertini, for instance, and among the youngest some very promising ones such as David Atherton and Andrew Davis. To me, the most helpful presence on the podium was my great and beloved master, Georges Enesco. He was so all-knowing, so infinitely helpful, that I always had the feeling that nothing could go wrong as long as he was there. Perhaps the most fantastic bit of accompanying I ever experienced was Enesco in Carnegie Hall accompanying a *very* nervous and erratic Symphonie Espagnole (Lalo) played by a very young Spanish violinist.

Before he plays, the violinist should not tarry too long in acknowledging applause. This applause is a greeting; it is not yet a tribute.

And when it comes to accepting an audience's tribute the violinist should neither discourage nor too obviously encourage. He must genuinely feel grateful to his audience, grateful that they have come, grateful that they have understood, appreciated, and received what he has given them.

The performer should take them all in and move quickly from one face to another, so that he almost looks at each one individually in turn. If there is a particularly beautiful woman sitting on the stage or in the audience, he must not look at her more – or only a very little more – than at anyone else! He must make up by looking to others in her vicinity.

If the soloist's success is such that he is recalled many times, the conductor must be brought along at least every other time. At the first recall the conductor quite properly usually asks the soloist to go out alone.

The first recall with conductor is usually the moment for the conductor and soloist to ask the orchestra to share in the tribute by standing up. Standing up can be a delightfully ambiguous gesture, as it may sometimes be meant as a tribute to the soloist, especially when he comes on stage before he begins to play, and sometimes after the performance on the fourth or fifth recall it may be an opportunity to bring the concert to an end and a hint that the orchestra would like to leave!

Under no conditions should the soloist play an encore unless he has first consulted the conductor and, if possible, the first violinist. Usually the orchestra is thrilled to listen. At other times, when it is already late or the players are on tour or have trains to catch, the orchestra should not be held up. Sometimes the management is terrified lest the concert may run overtime. If the audience keeps on applauding until after the orchestra has been allowed to leave the stage and if the soloist feels up to it, he may then play another encore. No encore should be too long, out of deference for public transportation late at night, unless the occasion is such that anything is allowable!

If the soloist is placed before the end of the programme, i.e. if there is a piece to follow, he (or she) should not allow a success to carry on too long and thus spoil the conductor's finale. The same applies, though a little less crucially, when playing before the interval. Should the work include an important solo by a member of the orchestra, as for example the oboe solo in the slow movement of the Brahms Concerto, the soloist should ask the orchestral soloist to rise and take his bow immediately the work is over, after shaking hands with the conductor and the leader.

Above all, the soloist must feel a great sympathy with all the other musicians and convey to them a sense of respect and expectation.

There is a certain routine that I like to follow before a concert.

First of all, I find it important not to eat too much during the day; nothing that takes very long to digest or is heavy on the system. If the concert is at 8 o'clock I wake up from my sleep at about half-past four or five. I stretch, wash, do my exercises and warm up quietly, unless I leave my warming up for the concert artists' room back stage. At about half-past six, before going to the concert, I usually take a hot drink, milk or yoghurt, a tablespoonful of something like soya malt as a nourishing strengthener, and perhaps some vitamins – various preparations which I alternate or take as I feel like. I like to arrive about an hour and a half, or at least an hour, before concert time, to be one with the atmosphere, and to avoid interrupting this stage of my preparation with a car trip or any other travel.

I would also like to say a word about the mental attitude

which should be cultivated before and during a performance.

Having mastered his work, the violinist should enjoy a happy and eager anticipation, for he conveys a state of mind to the public, and when he walks out on the stage he achieves both a physical and spiritual impact. He need not be aggressive, but his stance and posture must be commanding. He must convey a certain ease and balance and communicate the commitment and precision of his thoughts and motions. He must impress his audience with the fact that he is at one with his work.

The public, it must always be remembered, is incidental and accidental to the music. If the violinist is in his music, the listeners will follow. He must never put the public ahead of his music. If he does that he can only lose the public. But if he masters the music he will master the audience – and will be able to hold them, stilled in concentration, on the single thread of a barely audible pianissimo.

But even with the best preparation the artist must not expect to be guaranteed inevitable and complete satisfaction. In fact, the greater the artist, the higher the vision in the knowledge of his own maximum capacity, the more glaring the gap – however small it may be – between the actual achievement at the concert and that supreme conception which he carries in his mind and heart.

Various unexpected things may happen in the course of a performance. A string may break, usually the E string, for that is the most fragile. Once, in the course of the Brahms concerto with orchestra, two E strings gave way during the first movement – one, which I changed, not long after the violin entry, and the second during the cadenza. I then exchanged my violin for the concert master's and carried on; by the end of the first movement he had put on a new E string, which orchestra members have the habit of carrying in their pockets. Somehow this in no way interfered with the communication of the music and, in fact, one often finds that the public enjoys an accident and the unexpected, if it is well and deftly handled and does in no way upset the performance.

Of course I would be very unhappy if a string broke, for example, in the middle of the slow movement of the Beethoven concerto. I think I would begin the movement from the beginning again; or, if it happened after the second tutti, I would resume the movement from the beginning of the second tutti. I would equally be unhappy if a string broke in the middle of Bach's *Chaconne*, where the build-up is such that the climax would be completely lost. It is such a tightly knit structure that it must exist unbroken from the beginning.

Another accident could be a memory slip. The very first time I played the Brahms concerto in public, when I was twelve and playing it with Verbruggen in Minneapolis, in the sixth bar of the solo violin entry of the slow movement I suddenly could not remember how it went on. Of course I stopped. I went over to the the conductor's desk and looked at the score; we resumed from the solo violin entry and carried on without further incident.

Sometimes, if the conductor and orchestra are on their toes, they may be able to cover up. But it is probably better to admit to an error, look it up and begin anew. It is, after all, a failing that may happen rarely, but it occurs within the chances of human frailty. A sudden distraction, a momentary loss of control or concentration, a physical, spiritual or emotional anxiety, perhaps low blood pressure, a tummy not functioning properly, the hall too hot, low vitality – or simply a complex work which has not yet yielded its last secrets, or been played enough, or reviewed in sufficient calm, or worked at in sufficient concentration – various pressures can bring about such a failing.

Among other causes that contribute to a failing of memory are the perturbations of body time that happen so often in our jet era when we fly vast distances from east to west and west to east. For several days after such a trip it is impossible to feel normal, and this affects not only coordination, mental and physical, but also emotional capacities. Such disorientation does not apply so much when travelling from north to south.

The recitalist with piano

The violinist giving a recital with a piano faces a specific problem – where to stand. I always feel that there is a great advantage for the violinist who plays at the bend of the piano. It takes a little getting used to, because the violinist hears the piano much louder than he does when he stands in the usual position behind the pianist. But on the other hand the balance of volume for the public is likely to be better because the pianist hears a little less of the violinist and cannot afford to play too loudly. And the violinist is immersed in the total sound of the composition, his own and the piano's sound coming from the same direction. This is, of course, especially necessary in sonatas where the piano and the violin are equal in importance.

In small pieces the lid can be put down to the shorter stick but when the violinist stands in the bend of the piano he profits from the resonance of the piano strings and the sound that emanates from a completely open piano lid.

Sometimes in halls with rather dead acoustics, and when playing solo sonatas of Bach, Bartók and some other composers, I stand in the bend of the piano, with the lid wide open and have a flat longish piece of metal inserted in the pedals which, passing under the middle pedal, holds the other two pedals down. This lifts the dampers off the piano strings and allows them to vibrate in sympathy with the violin sound. This has a wonderful effect and the violin sounds more as if it were played in a cathedral – as it should in these solo works.

Another advantage of this position is the violinist's contact with the pianist. The pianist sees the violinist and the violinist can look to the pianist for particular beginnings and attacks and, in fact, for that continuous *rapport* which is required when playing together. Standing behind the pianist can convey a disjointed relationship, as if two people, one with his back to the other, did not actually care about each other.

As I hinted above, the compact source of sound is important in its diffusion to the public. The sound reaches all parts of the hall as one sound, rather than as two separate sounds which do not always reach the extreme corners at the same time or with the same volume. The visual angle to the public is also better. The piano can be astride the middle of the space available; otherwise, with the violinist standing behind the pianist, the whole bulk of the piano is on one side of the stage. Thus the audience can both hear and see better, the instruments are better centred, and the artists are in closer contact with each other.

I used to play in the traditional position behind the pianist and sometimes do so even now, when it is too difficult to move the piano if I find it placed in the old established position, especially if there are stage seats, since standing in front of the open lid prevents the people behind the piano from seeing the violinist. But the only advantage to the violinist of standing behind the piano is that he can if need be – if he is not too sure – steal a glance at the pianist's music. And even this is of no avail if the pianist plays from memory!

The contemporary world

Perhaps the greatest satisfaction of the interpreting musician is to achieve that unique meeting of mind and heart with a flesh-and-blood contemporary composer. This can happen when that hitherto unknown human being, the composer, his soul bared, is gradually exposed for the first time in unambiguous sound, by the searching interpreter. The interpreter, whose normal role is recreative, comes closest to genuine creativity when he is alone with the composer and when, in the whole world, they are the only two who share together the first glimpse of their newborn work. Of course, the interpreter who also composes (as did, for example, Georges Enesco, or the great Italian violinists, not to speak of pianist giants such as Liszt, Busoni or Chopin) is among the really privileged.

But even in the humbler role, it is the union of understanding which brings particular fascination and fulfilment, the sense of being *essential* to another human being and earning his, or her, gratitude. One might expect composers to be exacting and harsh, yet in my experience they are able to hear an interpreter's intentions even before he, or she, can satisfactorily translate them into a mature performance.

The modern violinist cannot afford to entertain too many prejudices. Of course his temperament, his background, his upbringing, his training may predispose him to a particular style of music, a particular type of musical activity. It is important to cultivate a certain specialization. Up to a point it is important to go in depth into a certain style – say Bach or jazz. But at the same time we live in an era which demands that the enlightened player be open-minded – for it is only through curiosity, interest and study that we can get to know the genius of other musical people, different styles, extraordinary expressions as varied as the plumage of birds.

To the young violinist considering his prospects for the future let me say, first of all, that the violin should not be studied as a means of earning money. That may or may not come incidentally, but violin playing should be considered as an activity that enriches life. As I have said so often, some of the most successful people I know – bankers, merchants, industrialists, politicians, diplomats – are all people who have studied and played the violin and known when to give it up as a career. Most violinists from our schools go on to become part-time amateurs.

However, a good violinist can earn quite well today. There are not enough of them about, and in the orchestras and in the teaching profession there is a demand for quality.

We have seen that the violinist covers the whole gamut from hermit to the most gregarious of beings; from the lone student who works in isolation, as far away as possible from neighbours who would be disturbed and irritated, to the member of the orchestral team. The solo violinist plays pieces for violin alone, concentrating on endless exercises and caprices; the chamber music player joins and works together with a few beloved or sympathetic colleagues; the violinist in an orchestra is part of a body, a collective and fairly large group.

And it is here, in the orchestra, that we find one of the foremost uses of the violin. It is the violins – together with the other stringed instruments – which have always constituted the core and foundation of the orchestra. And it is on the violin, therefore – on all the stringed instruments, but primarily on the violin – that our musical heritage rests. We would not have a civilized life without our musical heritage, and that means without the violin.

Critics

Critics are the verbalizers of music. Their main task is to convey the meaning of a performance, the quality and the value of an artist and his efforts, not only to the public who have not attended the concert but to those many who have attended and want another view.

Fortunately there is no such thing as one opinion only, and nothing is more amusing than reading contradictory reviews by equally competent critics, for after all the critic himself – especially the music critic – is a subjective judge. He must be in the mood; the occasion must be right; he must feel that the work speaks to him even though he may have heard it a thousand times; he is, perhaps, harassed and pressed for time; he may have a bad seat. He may not like, for one reason or another, a particular composer; he may take an aversion to a particular style of playing which, valid in itself, may not appeal to his temperament – and conversely he may find something quite wonderful and astounding that might fail if he heard it again a day later.

Of course, all listeners must be free to form their own subjective judgements, and critics can be no exception.

There are exceptionally gifted critics who are versed in musical literature, who come prepared, who have studied scores and listened to recordings. But even they can never really account for the *reason* for a particular performance, good or bad; they can only discuss the final product. The best of them, by definition, cannot truly understand what went behind a particular performance. This is perhaps fortunate, because we would not necessarily want our most intimate and private motives and inclinations, weaknesses or strengths, revealed to the public.

It is amusing, however, that often when critics venture on to the shifting sands of elucidation (unless it be an obvious thing, like a string that is out of tune because of the weather or because it is new), their arguments from the viewpoint of the performer are frequently wrong.

It is best to know oneself: to listen to oneself with extreme attention, to judge oneself objectively and critically. Never worry about what critics might say, above all never allow them to influence your approach to music or your state of mind.

Finally, I advise you not to answer your critics' reproaches in print. I remember one exception, however, to which I must confess, which was too tempting to resist. We cannot, really, say: 'This is the way Bach wanted it.' But when one critic took me to task for the particular type of slide in Bartók's Second Concerto, which always begins at the beginning of the first note and not, as is usual, at the end of the first note, I had to write to tell him that this *was* the way Bartók wanted it.

Seven
Repertoire and Interpretation

Once in Lucerne, talking to Furtwängler, I heard him compare the interpretation of a work to the flow of a river, the interpreter to the man in the boat carried along by the stream. Sometimes the water rushes in a torrent through a narrow gorge, sometimes it spreads out to the serenity of a broad river flowing slowly through rich agricultural land.

Of course Furtwängler was a classic romantic, and he was indeed carried by the music. He allowed the music to fulfil itself. He was playing works that were the great heritage of the finest German tradition, known to excellent orchestras and to all musicians. He therefore allowed these works to breathe. He encouraged and inspired musicians to play these pieces as each of them knew that they should be played. He did not have to be the locomotive and master. He did not direct the river; the river was there. He merely guided the boat to avoid the roughest rapids and to arrive at the final destination.

Even when a work demands constant direction and control – even when a very contemporary, complex piece is unfamiliar to the musicians who have to play it – it is still a fine work if it conveys the listener, in an unbroken continuity of time, from one scene, one sensation, one mood, one state of being, to another, either by contrast or by evolution. Built-up tension can break; serenity can be prolonged until sudden impatience erupts; mounting tension – as in that tremendous build-up in the *liebestod* in *Tristan* – can slowly and gradually achieve a climax which can be quite shattering.

Above all music is the art of time. Where the sculptor handles clay or stone and the painter the visual symbol of the scene in his forms and colours, the musician handles time and makes it flow in different moods, makes it pass jerkily or smoothly, quickly or slowly, with intensity. And whether it is the harsh reality of existence or, as it were, a dream world, it is always time unbroken.

Thus to establish credible continuity we must search for the cells – the single cells, the germ cells – in melodic, rhythmic and harmonic elements which evolve, multiply, gain in complexity and are in fact building blocks which provide the material for any given place, any given work. These cells are the carriers of our inherited, instinctive, intuitive knowledge, of the wish-thought and of the memory-thought. They provide the inspiration and the mastery of the composer, or even of the composer–improviser who plays what he feels the moment he conceives it rather than setting it down in notation.

Such inspiration and mastery are what make of a work an eternal, priceless treasure.

Analysis

The advantage of the improviser over the musician who has learned to read and play the notes he sees on the music stave is that the improviser is usually carried by the stream of consciousness. His music, his sounds, will often be more convincing, will go to the core of his listener more naturally, just as the man who speaks from his heart without a text – if he is a good speaker – can reach his audience more directly than the one who has come with a prepared speech and just reads that text, regardless of audience reaction, regardless of the mood and feeling, the inclination of the moment.

Similarly, the violinist who plays a work from memory may convey – if he is playing the piece with the conviction and intelligence and understanding it requires, and if he has mastered his instrument – rapturous improvisation to his audience, as if those notes which he has studied for so many years still reveal, at the very moment when he is playing them again, a new secret, something which has just come to him, a new meaning which is particularly relevant to that very audience, to that very moment. This is perfectly possible, but to achieve this quality of communication with a great classic it is necessary to enter completely into the composer's mind, to follow his thoughts and his pen as he wrote those notes down, to follow evolution and impulses which carried him from one note to the next.

To do this I have evolved a personal system which I apply to every work. Stated shortly, it is that in analysing a work I do not give too much attention to the 'skeleton' – that is, the overall structure, exposition, development, recapitulation, coda, gross modulations, first and second theme, etc. We all know what a skull looks like and it is not the flesh of the living head, the burning eyes, the charming contours, the flowing hair, the speech and sound of the voice. And so these structural, skeletal, constituent parts are, however important, not the elemental part of my analysis.

Similarly, such labels as notes and harmonies are very useful to know and to identify (as important to learn as the grammar of a language). But – essential as this kind of knowledge is – its cultivation should not form a major part of the type of analysis I have in mind.

The French *solfège* method, disciplined and intellectually satisfying as it is, the ability to recognize and name any chord – its various inversions, its harmonic progressions – this is not everything. I would like to contribute a form of analysis which proceeds from the first note to the last of a composition, which does not accept any labels, but rather explains each note in terms only of its consequence as logical succession to the notes which preceded it in that composition.

Thus a D major scale in the Beethoven Concerto for Violin is no longer a D major scale. Why, a D major scale is simply any D major scale that you may practise any morning when you play your scales, on a violin, or on a piano! It does not represent the Beethoven Concerto for Violin. To understand the D major scale that happens to be a succession

of D, E, F sharp, G, A, B, C sharp, D in the context of the
Beethoven Concerto for Violin, it has to be explained by the
notes which preceded it and every element, every succession
between the D and the E, and E and the F sharp, etc.; the
rhythm of the scale, the particular rhythm in which it is
presented; the harmonies which may or may not be applied;
the speed of the rhythm which carries it. Such are the elements which constitute this particular form, which I have
evolved for myself, of analysing the music.

It is the difference between the analysis of a corpse, which
has been the stand-by of anatomy for so long, and the
analysis of the living structure, the pulsating cells, the blood
as it actually flows in the veins; this is totally different. It is
the opposite of a cold analysis. It moves me, as I study the
score, to the very depths of inspiration, of feeling, of astonish-
ment. I feel the same, almost, when studying the piece as
when playing it.

In fact while playing the concerto I progress along that
same well-prepared track. Of course I have no more time
than it takes to play the piece. By that point the additional
time taken in studying and analysing the work is no longer
available, but I am carried along on the stream of the
composer's own thought.

This analysis may seem ludicrous to certain people, who
say that the composer probably just wrote the music down.
But that is a nonsensical argument for I am actually hearing
the piece not as a finished work but in conception, and it
carries with it the myriad inflections, the myriad intentions –
even those unwritten, unspoken – which the composer had
in his mind and which took the particular form, the particular
harmonic sequence, the particular rhythmic structures, which
characterize that work.

Only thus can a work be played with conviction and
can it retain an ever-renewed freshness of conception. Only
thus can it reveal new facets when it is repeated.

'Distortion and correction'

One important method of perfecting interpretation is what I

call the process of distortion and correction. Essentially it consists of practising the work in this sequence. First decide which notes are the most important, which stresses should be underlined, where minute alterations of volume and speed would be called for, and exaggerate them. Then eliminate them, smooth them, plane them down, work at them with metronome, so that nothing remains obvious, nothing shows. The public, the listener, cannot say: 'He's deliberately twisting the phrase in this or that way', because what remains is essential and discreet, and reveals the line and the shape, the living ebb and flow.

Discretion is so important in all works, even the most wildly romantic. If you hear the *great* Russian musicians perform Tschaikovsky – and to what fantastic effect – you realize that the true way of making music – even with Tschaikovsky – is not to exaggerate but to allow the flow to carry you and to build up, without wilful twisting or distortion. A greater climax can be better built up by a relentless, continuous motion than by small excursions which lose the accumulated tension and dissipate the mood instead of allowing it to follow its creative course.

I believe that the play between freedom and discipline, between distortion and correction, must continue. There is no such thing as settling for one or the other. The one is life and the other is order. The one is inspiration and the other is form, and meaning, and elegance, and presentation. The one is wild and the other controlled, and they must continually be put into balance. The wild must not be allowed to erupt, and go off the handle, and carry us to extremes, nor the controlled be allowed to deaden, kill, make rigid and make useless our efforts at communication. The one is the fuel and engine, the other the driver or the pilot. The one is the wings, the other the eyes and the brain of the bird.

Memory

Memory feeds memory. Throughout our lives our recollections and awarenesses multiply each other reciprocally, resulting in variants of ever greater complexity, sensibility and clarity on any given experience. These very experiences link up and relate to each other: hence a huge bank of which no single element is disconnected. (Unique experience does occur, of course – on first listening to the Eroica Symphony, first love, etc.) Eventually, however, the painter, say, acquires a vast palette of colours which he can recognize, recollect in his mind's eye, name and reproduce at will. He also acquires a 'feel' for the meaning and expression of line. In this way he is better prepared to recall a fleeting image than the layman.

Some people have a natural eye, a natural ear. Such musicians can whistle or 'hear' for their lifetime tunes they may have heard only once. Improvisation, sheer emotional and physiological exuberance, what the Germans call 'Ubermut', motor satisfaction, and rare associations contribute to this spontaneous memory. At the other end of the spectrum are those who can only learn from a written or printed score. We may partake in degree of both. Best of all is to remember instantly, forever; but this is given to very few people – Mozart, Enesco . . .

For me, the first stage of the memory process is understanding. I have to clarify both the smallest elements of detail and the largest elements of overall form. Having analysed the work and tried to follow the composer's own path and vision, I couple that inner sound with the living sound. In the case of violin-playing, this means the feel of fingers and limbs, the emotional sequence, and even the aspect of the page. Memory thus gradually absorbs and condenses into a palpable, tangible certainty vague and fleeting impressions and their associated sensations.

Contemporary works are sometimes more recalcitrant. The styles are less conventional, forms freer, complexities multiplied, sounds and effects novel and unorthodox. They may take that much longer to become assimilated, digested into the unconscious and etched with bright clarity in the conscious.

Since Toscanini particularly, many conductors have dispensed with the score when conducting in public (some whilst playing an almost new score, even at rehearsal, as Mitropoulos and Maazel). But this is a matter of the individual, the score and the occasion, and I feel the decision should be flexible. The individual should follow his good judgement and instinct to determine each separate case. Some conductors (such as Toscanini who was appallingly short-sighted) have difficulty in seeing clearly. Others out of simple joy of abandon to the music and the performers, feel freer without stand or score; while some keep the score continuously before them and are no less great for that.

As a sensible convention, the conductor should in general (exceptions allowed) keep the score of the concerto on the desk whenever accompanying a soloist. Chamber music is usually played from the score, particularly in the case of string quartets. There are exceptions. Certainly the violinist on the stage, when standing alone, makes a better impression when he is not facing a music-stand, glued to the printed page, particularly if he must wear glasses. However, a beautiful performance is the be-all and end-all of music and takes everything in its stride. Some great pianists (and outstanding musicians) nearly always used the music – Myra Hess and Clara Haskil, for example – with no loss of communicative power or conviction.

For my part I think of music as improvisation, even in the case of a Bach Fugue, and my ideal is to hear it and play it as the composer might have created it, or as an Enesco or Ravi Shankar might improvise it.

Improvisation

Music began with improvisation. Then only gradually did notation become more precise and more exact. When notation was still in its early stages in the West, our musicians knew how to embellish what was in effect a kind of shorthand; they knew the conventions which the composer had in mind and which he did not trouble to write down – and which were in fact impossible to write down. If you listen to a gypsy violinist playing his incredible improvisations and ornamentations of any given melody or harmonic progression or sequence, you listen in amazement, for no human notation is sufficiently accurate to put down in notes the exact rhythm – even the exact pitch – of those sounds; it is quite impossible. It is something as natural, as phenomenal, as incredible and overwhelming as the song of a bird.

Notation has in fact reduced our range of expression by making us keep to certain notes at certain places; and if we have a legal and bureaucratic frame of mind we sometimes cannot give those notes the meaning the composer intended. The musicians who interpreted the works of the Middle Ages and the seventeenth century knew that the composer's indications were but the landmarks on the road they hoped the traveller would follow. They hoped you would take in the scenery and feel the mood of the countryside and would not merely register mileposts.

Ornamentation used to be a very great art which singers, violinists, and harpsichord players – in fact all musicians – indulged in and continued until fairly recently. A certain amount of ornamentation and improvisation is necessary, for example, for playing Handel. Nothing duller can be imagined than an authentic rendering of a Handel violin sonata, playing only the notes that are written down.

Improvisation in the form of cadenzas survived until relatively recently. In all Mozart concerti, for example, the soloist is expected to comment on the movement he is playing in a musical way, to recall certain features which have struck him, to embellish upon them, but always to remain faithful to the source of his inspiration, the actual thematic, rhythmic, harmonic, constituent elements of the movement. The composer entrusted him with these comments.

And even in the works of so authoritative a composer as Brahms, who lived at the turn of our century, the Romantic era, the soloist's comment is expected. He is expected to provide an elaborate cadenza in proportion to the size of the movement, and his cadenza occurs nearly always at the very end of the movement and is followed by the coda or, as in the case of the Mozart concerti, a short tutti.

Mendelssohn, however, perhaps distrusting the performer, and not wanting his work to be spoiled by an irrelevant or unworthy cadenza, wrote his own cadenza in the first movement of his concerto and placed it just before and leading into the recapitulation. His was an original mind in advance of his time, and more and more since his day composers have written their own cadenzas for the performer to obey.

But improvisation is still essential to communication, even when you play works long known to performers and to the public. To this end you cannot afford, while practising, to repeat, and repeat, and kill a work by consuming your inspiration. It is preferable to analyse the piece, to understand it, to master it; and then to work on the technical requirements, either in deliberately contrived exercises which isolate the difficulty and so help you to overcome the obstacle, or by playing with regard only to the flow of the physiological and physical sensation, the smooth changes of position, the bow changes, the evenness of sound, the evenness of rhythm. Usually I do this with a mute on the violin so as not to take away from the joy I will have, at the actual performance, of hearing myself, so as not to tire aural nerves, or to use up my emotion or my passion.

The problem of texture, of faithfulness to the score versus freedom of expression depends, to a certain extent, on fashion. If you listen to old recordings of Hoffman, for instance, or Ysaye, and of some great pianists, you will find a very great latitude of personal interpretation and therefore a very general intensity of communication. Later, after the First World War, we entered the more disciplined era of interpretation, and in the hands of people like Toscanini it was still a remarkable achievement of communication; but in the hands of imitators – who dotted their i's and crossed their t's – classical music lost a great deal of its meaning, and today in certain countries, among certain groups of musicians, Beethoven has been all but killed.

As I said above, the element of improvisation is still a vital part in the violin playing of gypsies, of traditional India, of Africa from which developed jazz. It has been one of my greatest delights to meet Stefan Grapelli, that wonderful jazz fiddler, who improvises with a facility and with an extraordinary sensitivity of imagination, who can embellish any melody and play variations of every description according to his fancy. It is almost impossible to write down what he plays. The style is profoundly personal and conditioned by jazz traditions, yet it is a style which can be imitated by others who have been introduced and bred to these traditions and conventions, have worked with musicians like Grapelli; and these others might conceivably develop another personal style, one which would be in keeping with the basic jazz, equally individual, and equally amazing.

The Western fiddler is usually taught from the printed page and this accounts for much of the dullness of Western violin teaching. We need to regain our capacity for inventiveness.

Yet the other extreme could be as dangerous. Marcel Ciampi, now over eighty, the great piano teacher in Paris, told me that in his younger days before the First World War no one would dream of questioning a personal interpretation: if someone asked 'Why do you play a particular passage in a particular way?' it was thought sufficient to answer: 'That's the way I feel it'.

A tug of war exists between order and chaos. Some people will always feel that it is a holy duty to create chaos, if merely to destroy order; others will feel that it is a holy duty to impose order, if merely to prevent chaos. Music – like all beauty, like civilization itself – is, and can be, a balanced state between these two extremes.

To take a supreme example: nothing is more romantic, elegiac, than certain of the preludes of Bach which precede the rigorous form of his fugues. In fact Casals has said that the prelude to the G Minor Sonata for violin alone, like a cadenza, was improvised, and the forerunner of the chromatic fantasy and fugue. Bach probably improvised many such on the organ, just as organists maintain to this very day a tradition of improvisation.

111

Part One: The Violin
The versatility of the violin

The violin has been, and still is, the most universal of stringed instruments. It is also the most perfect, having reached its perfection in the hands of the great violin makers of Cremona, and in the hands of the great violinists of Italy. We must never forget the contributions to the violin of 'bel canto' and of the operatic and dramatic traditions of Italy. When we think of Corelli, when we think of Tartini, of Locatelli, of Nardini – all the great and numerous violinist-composers of Italy – and finally when we think of Paganini, we realize what an enormous debt we owe the civilization of Italy and its sunny, singing, passionate, people. Such composers as these have written the basic works with which all students of the violin should become acquainted.

There are, of course, many styles of violin playing and of violin music. The violin is very suited to gypsies, that nomadic people who expressed the wild way of life and knew the stars of the night and every corner of the countryside, the wild sounds of the birds and all the animals, their own yearnings and nostalgia. They are said to have come from India.

The violin is at home in the classical music of India, having been adopted two centuries ago because it was superior in perfection and flexibility to the bowed stringed instruments native to India.

The violin is at home on the moors of Scotland, on the plateaux of Norway, in the Blue Ridge Mountains of America. The violin is at home in each Russian, Polish, and Rumanian village, where it has always accompanied the dancing and the singing.

Violins have been made of every description, crude and rough hewn, barely recognizable and yet quite adequate for the astonishing variety of roles they undertake. I have seen the gnarled, clumsy, horny fingers of Scottish bee keepers and sheep grazers playing Scottish reels, strathspeys, dances and laments with never a faltering rhythm or a wrong note, but perfect pitch and perfect rhythm. In fact the rhythm of folk people, whether in Russia, Hungary or Scotland, is always

112

superior to that of the urban, industrial, commercial civilizations of Western Europe.

The violin is so flexible an instrument that it evolves in each country according to that country's genius. It plays Tschaikovsky and the passionate virtuoso romantics if it is in Russian hands; it plays the 'bel canto' for an Italian; it plays the great musical literature of the classic German and Austrian heritage in those countries and, in fact, universally. And it was the instrument for which Purcell and Dowland wrote perhaps the most wonderful music of all.

I have a particular feeling and love for the music of the sixteenth century which proceeds with an intricacy of line, an absence of bar lines, a complexity of texture which can only be described as organic. Later music can be said almost to have degenerated into square, triangular rhythms, divided by bar lines and counterpoint; to have, with its inflexible rules, reduced the free flow of voices, and contained the modulation and the chromaticism in which the keyboard instruments (later to take over the leadership of music) could not indulge. Harmony, the evolution of counterpoint, was initially a predominantly vocal art which flowered from plainsong in the art of the chancel, and therefore is more closely linked to the violin than to the keyboard instruments, because it is only the stringed instrument that can adjust pitches sufficiently to achieve a counterpoint which is absolutely in tune. In fact the ability to modulate between keys was only made possible on the keyboard instruments by the invention of the tempered scale. And I would hazard an historical guess that this tempered scale could never have happened were it not for the stringed instruments which were guided by the ear and could, in fact, use quarter tones (and far smaller intervals even) and remain always perfectly in tune regardless of the pitch or key of the melody. The violin probably contributed more to the advent of modulated chromatic harmony than the piano, or the precursor of the piano, the harpsichord.

The music of Purcell and Dowland, dating back to a time when the voice and particularly the stringed instruments were more important than the keyboard, indulges in an extraordinarily rich chromaticism and in a continuity of sound which the voice itself cannot achieve because of having to breathe every so often, and which only a stringed instrument can produce. It is no wonder that this rich English heritage is being rediscovered and is reinvigorating the musical life which is flowering in the most remarkable way in the England of today.

Bach

At this stage I would like to consider one of the foundations of the violinist's repertoire: Bach's six sonatas and partitas for violin alone.* Here the instrument is used in its fullest capacity, in the most complete possible way – for the violin alone represents melody, counterpoint, harmony. In fact nothing is missing from these master works when they are played as they should be. The range of expression is total. It extends from the most philosophical serenity, as in the Andante of the A Minor Sonata, requiring a rhythmic and a technical discipline of note lengths and string crossing which remains unsurpassed in all the violinist's repertoire to the most overpowering climaxes, as in the *Chaconne*. It includes the semi-improvised almost fantasia of the Adagio of the G Minor and the fugal forms where the strictest observance of voice leading, timing, relative values, and of course rhythm, is exacted. And from the single line, the single melodic line, to the most involved chordal requirements, as in the B Minor Suite or the *Chaconne* and the Fugues, to the contrapuntal, as particularly in the C Major Fugue with its accompanying voices, the chromatic line is heard with the theme.

But of all these qualities the overriding one is the sense of formality, of structure, of proportion. Climaxes must be graded. If there are several climaxes it is often necessary to decide which should be the louder. Sometimes in fact they are

*See also pp. 117 to 121, and Denis Stevens's essay which begins on p. 221.

equal. There are three climaxes in the *Chaconne* and I believe that they are all approximately of the same level of intensity, one occurring at the end of the first half, the end of the D minor part; another at the end of the D major part; and the third, of course, at the end. But the exacting requirement of a balanced structure must never be lost sight of in Bach. Speeds, dynamic levels, ritardandi, these can only be done within very measured proportions. A romantic ritardando is very elastic. But in Bach it should be done unobtrusively and at the very end of the composition, usually not the end of the first exposition but at the end of the second repeat, the final end of the movement, and even then extremely discreetly and soberly. It can also be done very slightly at the end of certain climaxes, say the D major climax in the *Chaconne* but never so as to interrupt the basic pulse of the piece.

The music of Bach also requires a very special stylistic approach. It is not music in which the performer indulges himself for himself. He does so on a very, very high level – on a level which is spiritual and emotional and yet from which the spiritual and emotional impurities have been extracted. Together with Bach, the devotional atmosphere of a very fervent religious conviction, and the faith of the whole congregation, the player submits his own person to the will of God. There is an element of exalted resignation and yet a strong personal will to unite with God, to assert Man's achievements, intellectual, spiritual and social. There is no lack of pride, of grandeur, but at the very same time there is humility and respect. This is something which is perhaps lost to our day for we look upon these qualities as antagonistic and mutually exclusive, but they are not and should never be. Where they are united in one person, as in Bach, as in any deeply believing person who takes pride in his responsibilities, in the fact that he can fulfil what he exacts of himself and what is expected of him, they produce a valuable, a balanced and a worthwhile person.

To be specific, the stylistic demands would exclude, for instance, very wide vibrato. They would also exclude slides – except in one or two places where they may be used with the utmost caution and more or less unobtrusively, almost unobserved, but lending a voice-like quality to a melodic line. But certainly the most important thing is to observe the clear and clean conduct of the individual voices. This also applies in the many movements which are only one voice, for that is only a superficial aspect, and there may in fact be two, three or four voices within that one voice so that, like a ventriloquist, the violinist on his four strings must continually change colour and strings to achieve this oral clarity. Usually – and this is the remarkable thing about Bach's mastery of violin technique – this is best achieved by playing in first position, sometimes shifting a half tone up to the second, but rarely in the upper positions – except where this is clearly unavoidable, as in the last movement of the C Major where the music goes up to the middle G on the E string of the violin, which has to be played in the sixth position. But otherwise the clarity of the leading voice is best achieved in the first position and it is a great mistake to indulge in flights of violin virtuosi exhibitionism on the G string, an indulgence which is too often attempted, and is in the worst bad taste.

Paganini

Perhaps as good a diet for the violinist as the six Sonatas of Bach are the twenty-four *Caprices* of Paganini. These too are masterpieces in their own way for they cover pretty well a very wide range of violin technique and they are calculated to make the violinist aware and to stimulate his technical and violinistic flair. They are all extremely musical and, in addition to that, they are so elegantly calculated as to bring the violinist along, to inspire him, to encourage him, to stimulate him to a maximum potential. They are also written for the violin to be played alone, though a few have been set to accompaniments more or less successfully. Enesco wrote a beautiful accompaniment to the *Trill Caprice* No. 6.

Incidentally when I play the Moses variations of Paganini, which are composed to be played entirely on the G string, I always tune my violin to give a maximum resonance. I tune the G string up to B flat, the D string to E flat, the A string to B flat and the E string down to E flat.* The violin sounds tremendous, with resonating sympathetic strings similar to those used so often in Indian instruments and ancient guitars.

In detail: Bach's D minor Partita and Beethoven's Violin Concerto

Interpretation is the art of projecting the essential unity of a work whilst 'living' every subtle shade of that continuous process in time which is music and is specifically the given lifetime of each work. Perhaps the germ-cell of music, as of life, is a particular pattern of vibrations, a particular pulse. It is subtle and flexible, but it is uninterrupted. There is, of course, another state of being which is seemingly without pulse (rhapsodic, for example, or meditative and dreaming) but even there I feel that the composer and the interpreter are in fact surrendering to a greater unity.

Take for instance the Preludes and Fugues of Bach. The Preludes are sometimes rhapsodic, as in the Chromatic Fantasy and Fugue, and usually improvisational in character; while the Fugues are rigorous and measured. The first is an evocation, the casting of a spell, a ritual of prayer and surrender; while the second is a disciplined, integrated structure in which the elements of rhythm, line and harmony are ordered.

I propose to touch on two great works in violin literature, the Violin Concerto of Beethoven and the D minor Partita of Bach. Here we can see these principles in action. The D minor Partita culminating with the Chaconne is a monumental structure, and shares with all great works the fulfilment of its promise and the sense of completion this always takes in the form of restatement, recapitulation, and duality which encloses the life-giving forces of the particular personality, the individual experience, of the composer.

Another element of continuity is provided by the three great climaxes which are achieved in the course of the *Chaconne*.

*As indicated by Paganini himself.

117

The rhythmic element is at its most melodic and least marked
at the beginning of the 25th bar. Here for one bar we have
six equal quavers and this, the quietest bar, marks the
beginning of a rise in intensity which reaches its high point
with the *forte* scale passages in demi-semi-quavers and falls
down again gradually to the very soft beginning of the
arpeggiato-chord on three strings. This is a gradual rise and a
gradual fall, but has not arrived at a climax. The first climax
is the end of the minor section which precedes the chorale
organ effect of the beginning of the section in major. Indeed
the very middle of the Chaconne happens four bars before
this section begins on a D major chord, which I always
observe with a form of reverence as one would a mile post
on the road.

The second climax, again *arpeggi* over four strings, precedes the return to the last section in minor. It will be noticed
that there are great, long, almost geological formations
leading from river beds to mountain crests but (although
there are sudden *pianos* when we arrive at a cliff edge and
then begin again several thousand feet below) there are never
any sudden *fortes*, as in Beethoven, following *pianissimos*.
The third and last climax is, of course, the very end.

The whole of the D minor Partita is in fact a constant and
ever-renewed building: it goes up and up and becomes more
and more magnificent without ever losing the human touch.
However overwhelming the size and sheer power, one never
forgets the compassion and the feeling for the suffering
individual in the music of Bach. It was Enesco who told me
that to do justice to the returning minor after the middle
section in major I should look at the statue of Riemen-
schneider. Perhaps no more fitting description of that passage
can be evoked than by the sad Madonna which can still be
seen in the Frankische Museum in Würzburg. The pain and
tragedy combined with a nobility and dedication is as true
of the statue as of the music.

In playing this work I love to play the whole Partita
without interruption, with just a short breather at the end of
the Gigue and before the Chaconne. To satisfy the demands

118

of unity and cumulative effect, however, I also do not alter the pattern of the *arpeggi* at the end of the D minor section, which Bach wrote out for only the first quavers. I keep the same pattern (his own) to allow this irresistible cumulative power to develop. I feel that what one risks with a change of pattern (very fashionable in the egocentric virtuosi period of the 19th century) is the distraction of the listener from the gathering climax and the reduction of the impact of the music.

Even though there can be no allowance in the music of Bach for arbitrary effects, personal indulgence, or changes of direction, as there are indeed in the romantic literature, there is every justification for a flexibility, a fluidity of line, a play of accent, colour and stress within a given series of notes, but only of course when these are justified by a sensitive and disciplined musical intuition and by an intellectual awareness.

For instance, although many of Bach's movements for solo violin and particularly for 'cello are written in one voice, that is without counterpoint and harmony, the counterpoint and the harmony are in fact implied and every effort must be made to bring the different voices out clearly, even though there is never more than one voice sounding at a time.

We must remember the organ on which Bach played and the limitations of the dynamic range within an organ stop. This expression could only be achieved by that infinitesimal variation of length of note which would give proportion and line to the pattern. It can perhaps be compared to a frieze which has little depth, perhaps only a few centimetres, but yet creates an illusion of three-dimensional perspective. On the violin the different strings can be made to fulfil different organ stops and the different voices allotted their particular strings. I think that, excepting in the very rarest of instances, the first position and the lower positions generally are the most suited to Bach's violin writing. I am convinced that Bach knew pretty well the fingering which the violinist would be using. The high positions, except for those notes which can only be played in the highest positions on the E string, are as thoroughly unsuited to Bach as they are suited indeed to Tchaikovsky. I do not mean to imply that in playing Bach's violin music we should not avail ourselves of the great expressive qualities of the violin, but we must do so with a sense of discretion and avoidance of all those character-istics of violin playing which are more suited to the romantic age. Wide vibrato, for instance, should be avoided and too great variations in tone or colour. However the minor in-flection, the minimal 'deviations', are absolutely essential to a sense of the living *work*.

I am equally opposed to the dry-as-dust Bach school which would reduce the music to a sterile, scholastic, uncommuni-cative and thoroughly dull performance.

In the fingerings required I favour the stretching from one position to another, playing as it were in two or even three positions at once. This I believe is very important to master and substantially it means a great control over the lateral stretch in the knuckles and the fingers of the left hand, for it is often necessary to reach back or forward for a low note on the G string which belongs to the bass voice, or for that mat-ter to find the intermediate voices on their appropriate strings.

I write this knowing that it is important to set down in words my reasoning. However, I would rather refer the reader to a performance. The most moving performances are those which I remember playing in the great cathedrals, for they were built with this particular music in mind. The solo violin generates waves of sound which envelop the listener in a building which itself is vibrating as one unit. I recall playing in Canterbury Cathedral and in many abbeys all over Europe from St Michel de Cuxa near Prades (which dates from I believe the 10th century) to Coventry Cathedral, from Westminster Abbey and St Paul's to our little mountain church in Saanen in Switzerland. There is no doubt that Bach's music is God's music.

To return to our Partita. The Chaconne is a work which, like all great works, depends on the unity and the cohesion of its presentation. In fact the whole power of the D minor Partita is a cumulative one and any interpretation not organically justified disperses completely the gathering thrust, the power, the magnificence of this edifice. Any arbitrary or wilful tampering is like the crack which may cause the building to crumble.

The Chaconne is a series of variations in dance form on four recurring and descending basic notes, but in performance it surmounts the variation form and does not in fact affect us as so many separate variations, but rather as an indivisible and continuous work of music. Bach uses various means to achieve this end. One is his recurrent practice of anticipating the first bar of a variation by the last bar of the previous one: already in the eighth bar of the piece we have a dotted rhythm, a dotted quaver and two demi-semi-quavers which anticipate the same rhythm in the succeeding bar on the same second beat. The pattern of the arpeggio variation in semi-quaver notes is anticipated one bar before the actual variation begins. The first complete variation in uninterrupted demi-semi-quavers in *piano* is anticipated in the bar before this begins.

This proof of continuity is in itself sufficient evidence that Bach would not have wanted any *ritardandi* at the end of variations. *Ritardandi* would impede the very purpose of this construction. The units are very often a double set of variations. Thus the variations often occur in pairs, that is instead of the variation having eight bars, there will be another variation, similar in rhythm, in feeling, or an echo, which gives us again larger units on which to establish our continuity, for example, the sixteen bars following the first eight.

With Beethoven the two pillars of exposition and recapitulation enclose the very personal expression contained in the development. But the whole of the First Movement of his Violin Concerto derives from the rhythmic impulse of the four tympani notes in the first bar (they are deliberately on the tympani for they are almost pure rhythm without melody, without harmony). This first measure propels the whole of the First Movement. There is a constant striving for a basic simplicity, for statements which are almost axiomatic in their self evidence, but which like all very great truths reveal themselves at the end of the struggle and not at the beginning.

121

This is perhaps the most important factor in the interpretation of Beethoven. One has to realize and to grasp the universal meaning of those truisms which remain as fundamental and as eternal as a law of nature, or a geometric theorem, or a quotation from Shakespeare or the Bible. Humanity rests on such eternities.

What appears as a simple scale in a work of Beethoven cannot be played as a labelled string of notes; and those who would play the D major scale in the wood winds at the beginning of the concerto simply as a D major scale have no idea of what Beethoven is about. In fact, to understand a work of Beethoven is to take this work as a living entity of which every expression and every evolution can only be explained by the notes and the moments which precede. In, for instance, the last melodic notes of the fourth to the fifth bar, C sharp, D, E **(a)** which resolve into D, E, F sharp at the beginning of the above movement wood wind scale **(b),** which reappear as three rising notes at the beginning of the Slow Movement **(c),** and in the Last Movement as the three last notes of the first half of the main melodic statement **(d)** – this is just one small clue to three notes which otherwise, deprived of their symbolic value, would be just three notes of the ascending scale.

(a) Allegro ma non troppo

(b)

(c) Larghetto

(d)

The Beethovenian process is, in fact, the inversion of most other developments. Mostly, development is a progression from the simple to the more complex, but in Beethoven it is a reduction of the bewilderment and confusion of whatever it is we apprehend to the crystallization and clarity of something which cannot possibly be further reduced; any further reduction and what we still grasp would totally vanish.

Take the third and fourth bars of the Slow Movement **(e)** and compare them with the opening bars of the Concerto and again with the solo violin restatement of these first bars in minor at the beginning of the development section after the second great tutti **(f).** You will notice that the Slow Movement is an evocation of the solo violin's restatement in minor of the opening tune, even to its resolution in the fifth bar; but, denuded of flesh, only the skeleton remains.

As a matter of curiosity just take a particular rhythmic element, or our three rising notes of the scale, and look through the whole work for the recurrence of these germ-cells.

Or, for instance, take the element of arpeggios – the first fortissimo in the first tutti **(g)** and the first solo violin's comment on the main theme as it enters in the Second Movement **(h),** or the very beginning of the Last Movement **(i).**

Take the wonderful melody which follows the long

perdendosi in the Slow Movement and which occurs again at the very end of the Slow Movement **(j).** This is a restatement of the melody in G minor in the development section of the First Movement **(k).**

It must be readily understood that an interpretation can only convey the music of Beethoven if it transmits what lies behind the notes: if the interpreting musician bears in mind the symbolic value of each note and can communicate it, without impediment, to the public. Any deviation, whether an ugly sound, a twisted rhythm, an incorrect stress, or a sudden arbitrary impulse, would destroy the magic which is in fact the communication of Beethoven. There is an explanation for every note of the piece, both on the intellectual and the affective level. Yet of course the violinist goes beyond both these levels (which must nevertheless be present) to another level which is that of the infallible. Here everything that happens happens because it is right, and must happen, and is not the result of thought or of deliberation, but of living the moment; one is carried by the life of the work and one's own complete identification with it. There is not a single note that does not carry its own right to live and which does not at the same time have a proportionate relation to all the other notes in its vicinity, whether in time or space.

Written instructions give the general indication of the composer's intent; we must always refer back to these to recheck accuracy and we must scrupulously observe them. But, beyond this alphabet and the words the notes spell out, there is a whole world of living expression which depends on the subtle and the reciprocal relationships between each of these myriad notes. The degree of deviation from the mathematically precise rendering of the score is for the most part infinitesimal. It can hardly be registered by even electronic testing instruments. Yet to compare a mathematically absolute precise performance with one in which the violinist achieves subtle inflections of changing light and shade and subtle rhythmic alterations in the most elusive differences between the lengths of notes is to compare life and death, the presence of Beethoven which can be evoked and his complete absence.

I could go on explaining in detail all sections of notes in this Concerto but, once the principle is understood, the reader can spend for himself rewarding hours and days analysing any great score. In the light of these examinations, he can discover the hidden meanings in every change of texture, every change of dynamics, whether gradual or sudden, every impetuosity, every hesitation, every fleeting remembrance, every noble show of determination or even of rage. Thus Beethoven lies revealed to us in his innermost depths, in a way which words, unless those of a poet, would be too cumbersome, too long-winded, too crude and clumsy, to convey.

Eight

The Making, Repair and Care of the Violin and Bow

Some famous violin-makers and their instruments

Two names deserve special mention in any study of the violin. The first is Stradivarius,* a dedicated *luthier* who worked fully and regularly over his long life, probably never missing a day, and who was as precise and exacting of himself as he was critical and exacting of his material. Joseph Guarnerius† on the other hand – a member of a family of renowned *luthiers* – worked in an erratic though inspired way. Every violin he made was a new creation. It seems that every one of his models was changed periodically. Every violin was a new inspiration, a discovery, an insight, and every violin had a different character. But all his violins have an earthy, gripping, deeply romantic and humanly touching quality.

I have been more than fortunate in my own violins, for I have had two most wonderful musical companions in two extraordinary Stradivarius violins. The first I have had since the age of thirteen, a violin which Stradivarius made when he was ninety years old – proudly noting this fact in his own handwriting on a label inside the instrument. It is a violin of warm, ample, strong and supple qualities, and was ideally suited to my youthful romantic approach. My second Strad. violin is an entirely different instrument. This was made in 1714, the *luthier's* so-called 'Golden Period', when he was seventy-one. This violin has enormous power, great brilliance, a purity and clarity of sound and a nobility of texture.

*Antonio Stradivarius of Cremona (born c. 1644).
†Joseph Guarnerius of Cremona (born c. 1666).

126

It is like a highly-bred racehorse, capable of the greatest feats of endurance, of brilliance, of self-discipline and control, and yet so proud and unbending as never to allow itself to be ridden by anything less than the lightest, most flexible touch. It is perfection and must be played to perfection.

Despite the sense of fidelity I have always felt for these Strad. violins I have always nurtured a hidden love for the Guarnerius instruments, and at various times in my career I have used Guarnerius violins. Each time it has been a moving experience, rich in satisfaction and stimulus. In particular I recall a month in 1931 or 1932 when I borrowed the Ysaye Guarnerius which now belongs to Isaac Stern and was at the time the property of Emile Français of Caressa and Français. It seemed to me that Ysaye's fingers were playing the violin and that I was merely shadow playing. And more recently, in 1968, I borrowed the D'Egville Guarnerius from Professor Lutz in Germany. This is one of the most famous and perfect of instruments, and it responded to my every inflection. Though slightly smaller than my Strads. it had terrific vitality, a richness of texture and enormous penetrating power.

Another *luthier* who has stood the test of time is Grancino.* His violins, somewhat like Amatis,† are not meant for great halls, but are exquisite instruments of great quality, and are ideally suited to the sound of intimate chamber music. My first really good violin, which I still have, was a 7/8 Grancino.

And we must not forget the contemporary violin-makers. I personally have a Cappichioni, a fine, strong and healthy instrument; another strong and beautifully constructed violin by the French *luthier* Paul Kohl; and two instruments by Smith in Sydney, one of which, an excellent violin, is a copy of my first Strad., the Prince Khevenhüller.

Each violin – or viola – has its own character and leaves an imprint on the player just as any companion will affect the

*Giovanni Grancino of Milan (born c. 1669).
†Nicolo Amati (born c. 1520), most famous of a famous family of violin makers in Cremona.

127

temperament, behaviour and way of thinking of his or her partner. So there is an interaction, an interchange of influence. A violin well played on will be liberated and will sound in a way that a badly played violin will never sound. After all, when several hours or more each day are spent with a particular object of beauty on which one's whole existence depends, there cannot but be a deep attachment, a sensitivity, a *rapport*, a feeling of oneness.

The bow

It would be wrong to speak of the violin without speaking of its essential accessory, the bow. This too is a priceless object and, ever since the great François Tourte* evolved the modern bow, has been a prized possession. The bow is like a knight's sword. It is a tool and it must feel right in the hand; it must have the right weight, resilience, flexibility, length and balance. It is something so very personal that violinists who have once used and liked a bow have almost never been known to give it up.

I have myself used for most of my career a beautiful Voirin, one which is much stronger than the average and which Enesco approved when I showed it to him in 1932. It came from Caressa and Français. Over the decades I have acquired many bows and now I am using a Dominique Peccate† which I bought from Vatelot in Paris about seven or eight years ago. It is slightly heavier and seems to fall between the Voirin and the Tourte. I still have the original Tourte, which came, as it were (the dealer threw it in), with the first Stradivarius that was given to me. It is hardly something that would happen today when a gold mounted Tourte can fetch $20,000.

The other day in recording baroque music I used a baroque bow, one of those which had been used since time immemorial, in that the arc of the bow was like the bow of the bow and arrow. It did not turn inwards towards the horsehair,

*François Tourte, b. 1810, in Paris.
†Dominique Peccate, b. 1747, in Mirecourt.

but outwards away from the horsehair. These bows are like butter in the hand. They are so very plastic and at the same time have such depth of resilience. It is like riding on very high springs instead of very taut springs. They can encompass three and even four strings at one time and at the same time they give the stroke a quality of definition, a sharpness, an incision which is not possible to achieve as easily with the modern bow.

The repair of the violin

A great tragedy of today is that there are very few violin-makers, or *luthiers* as they are called in France, to whom one can go with one's violins. Now that we have come to recognize the unique perfection of the great violins, their rarity has imposed a rising value on them. But the fact is that there are perhaps only a dozen violin repairers in the whole world who have the eye, the ear, the hand and the experience to touch, let alone repair, these instruments. As for adjusting a violin to its maximum capacity, this is an independent art and I myself know of only two or three people who can do it.

There are great violins all over the world which are badly looked after and will quickly deteriorate for lack of attention.

It is my personal conviction that our factories have taken our population too far away from the satisfactions of skilful manual techniques. On the whole workers do not complete any article themselves from start to finish; they do not express themselves; they do not receive the gratitude of those they serve. I am sure there are many young people who would love to give their lives to the satisfying work of a technique or craft – such as the making of violins, or fine furniture or books – if it could be recreated, re-instilled.

I am most anxious to encourage young people to become expert *luthiers*, and should like to start a school for training violin-makers and repairers. It is a very worthy and satisfying occupation, and one that yields great rewards. It engages the imagination; it gives joy through the practice of a craft of such perfection and delicacy; it demands tremendous intuitive intelligence to understand the requirements of each violin and each particular player.

The prices of ancient instruments are so astronomical as to justify a high price for their maintenance and repair – so much so that, sadly, this price is at present beyond the average violinist.

The care of the violin

The making and repair of violins may be highly skilled occupations, but every violinist can, and must, care for his instrument.

First and foremost I cannot sufficiently stress the importance of spotless cleanliness, not only of the violin, the finger-board, the strings, and the bow-stick, but of the violinist's own person and naturally, in particular, of his fingers and hands. Above all remember that a violin may be held only at the neck and the chin-rest, and no finger may touch the body anywhere else.

Alcohol and purified benzine or gasoline or eau de cologne may be used to clean the finger-board, but not a drop of this, nor any moisture on the rag, may touch the body of the violin or the varnish, for this would destroy the varnish. It is as important to keep the chin-rest clean (again with alcohol) as the finger-board, and for the same reason. You can get inflammation where the skin of your neck touches the chin-rest, and also get inflammation between your nails and fingers. It is merely a matter of cleanliness, and if the chin-rest and the finger-board are kept spotless, the strings as well, and your fingers and neck are kept well scrubbed – the fingers with a soaped brush – these irritations simply will not occur.

The strings may also be cleaned with refined gasoline, and alcohol, and sometimes during the course of a concert I use very fine metal floss to rub away the incrustation of resin on the strings. It is amazing how this deposit of resin inhibits the free vibration of the strings and how much clearer and bell-like the sound is as soon as this is removed. It accumulates with only ten minutes' playing, or even less, but obviously the rubbing away process can only be carried out between numbers.

I have such an aversion to the inevitable and essential but sticky substance of the resin that when I practise I almost always put a piece of tissue over the F holes directly under the pan of the bow, folding the edge over the two outer edges of the bridge, and placing a heavy five-pronged mute over the bridge to hold these two edges down. Thus the tissue, attached to the bridge, will not move away, and the violin itself is protected from the resin which falls on the tissue instead.

The body of the violin itself, its surface, can be cleaned by a variety of products. I use one prepared by Etienne Vatelot in Paris. It contains a very little water, cleans very well, and does no harm to the varnish.

This is essential because some polishes are too oily, others too abrasive or rough. These latter must never be used; nor are the oily ones, in their own way, much less dangerous for they penetrate the wood and deny it its vibrating freedom. Similarly, hard lacquered polishes which dry and form a stiff shiny surface are also bad, for they inhibit the vibration of the wood.

The inside of the violin may be cleaned by putting in a few grains of rice and shaking them around. Then, while shaking, invert the violin to allow them to drop out of the F holes. They will carry with them an accumulation of dust which very frequently will roll itself around the grains of rice and appear as a small ball of dust at the F holes, which can be drawn out with a little finger.

It is a sad fact that many violinists treat their violins badly; they do not look after them but allow sweat and resin to collect and mark the instrument and varnish. The varnish of these old instruments is something so unique and beautiful, so deep and velvety, so delicate, that it in particular must always be most carefully looked after. It must never be touched by hand, nor by alcohol or cleaning fluid; resin must never be allowed to accumulate on it and sweat, when it does form, must immediately be wiped away.

It is a pity that most contemporary varnishes are made on a base of alcohol rather than of oil. Alcohol naturally dries more quickly; but what is that span of drying time compared with the life of joy and pleasure that a beautiful violin can give generations upon generations of musicians and collectors? Alcohol varnish is cold and brittle, hard, unyielding.

Before putting your violin back into its silk bag, remember to clean the resin off the strings. Alternatively wrap tissues (held by the mute at the bridge) around the strings. Thus you will prevent the resin rubbing off against the inside of the silk bag, and eliminate the possibility of resin settling on the back of the violin if you ever slip it into the bag in a reversed position.

Before returning a bow back into its case, always release the tension of the hair and stick by turning the knob anti-clockwise at the frog end until the hair almost touches the stick.

The violin is not an instrument for all climates. It belongs to the temperate zones. The delicate wood and its adjustment do not hold up in conditions of extreme humidity or extreme dry cold – the North American continent, for instance, is suited neither to great furniture nor to great violins – but with care such dangers can be surmounted.

For dry winter weather I use wet 'snakes' which I insert through the F holes very carefully, dipping them in water every day to maintain the moisture. They are, of course, a poor replacement for a suitable climate, but they do make a great difference; I remember how much I used to suffer before these snakes were invented.

As for the tropics, it is only possible to survive in air-conditioned rooms and in air-conditioned concert halls, but even that is a very terrible artificiality. I, for one, do not take a violin to the hot, humid tropics if I can possibly avoid it.

Tuning. With regard to tuning the violin, it is best to reach the perfect pitch on a last upward turn of the peg clockwise. This way the string is likely to remain longer at pitch without

The Making, Care and Repair of the Violin and Bow

stretching or coming down in pitch. It is probably owing to the resistance at the top of the neck and at the bridge, which, on a downward turn of the peg, might distribute unevenly the string-tension over the three parts (above neck, main stretch, and below bridge) that unevenness tends to redistribute itself, thus lowering the pitch.

Nine
Teaching

Playing the violin is, I believe, a most exacting discipline. I would like to see it well taught, to all those who want to play but have had no opportunity and no introduction. This is, in fact, what I hope this book, and others in this series about other instruments, will help to achieve.

There is no doubt that the temperament which from childhood matches the demands of the violin is different from the temperament which for example finds fulfilment in the piano keyboard.

Yet violin students can be of an enormously wide variety. There is the born virtuoso; there is the more methodical, or humble, or reverent, young musician who just loves to make music. There is the music student who only wants to become acquainted with the violin as a stage towards becoming a conductor or composer, or simply to get the feel of the stringed instrument because he wants to become a musicologist and study ancient musical instruments, or hopes to be a violin maker or repairer. The teacher must learn to adapt himself or herself to them all.

Certainly teaching is the best way of learning, for it imposes upon the teacher the need for clarification, for justification, for thorough study, for demonstration.

The pupil, by definition, accepts; but it is no more than the seed that the earth accepts, for if it is to flower the seed must grow into a plant which gives. It is the giving which strengthens and makes one aware; it is the reciprocal communication which defines a character, a temperament, and a technique in its maturity. It is good to begin to teach as soon as you know something, but of course the greatest teachers are those who are experienced.

The student must be guided methodically through basic technique and all the stages of his learning. The technical, the musical, the improvisational stages must be taken step by step. But this is not enough. The teacher must also see to the posture, the health, the state of well-being of his charge. He must take eagle-eyed note of all visible and detectable manifestations of his pupil's character and temperament, and to a certain extent guide and mould them in the direction which best enhances performance. The precise and literal must be loosened and given romantic and exuberant quality and expression.

A constant line, a constant balance, must be maintained between criticism and encouragement. In fact ideally the two should be seen as synonymous, a balance between severity and *laissez faire*; for the student must discover things for himself, must be allowed to wander sometimes and yet must not waste too much time on mistakes or wrong paths. But it is his ability to correct himself which it is so important to cultivate, and the teacher must constantly avoid being satisfied with his own ready-made analysis and encourage the pupil to formulate thoughts, to explain the principles and to apply them on his own initiative.

The teacher must always be brought work prepared to the best of the student's ability. He must be looked upon as friend and counsellor, guide and authority – but an authority which does not freeze, rather releases and brings out. The student should always feel free to ask questions, to ask the why and the wherefore.

The pupil must always feel that the teacher's overriding purpose is to help him further his musical advancement, to serve the music. As long as this is clear, any passing impatience or even anger can be forgiven.

It is not necessarily always the older who instruct the younger. I encourage every child at my school who has acquired the grasp and the knack of some particular problem to convey it to his or her colleagues, younger and older. But, nonetheless, it is with growing age that teaching becomes deeply satisfying. I did not begin teaching formally until I felt I had sufficiently clarified my approach and understood things for myself to be able to communicate to others. But in another sense, from my earliest years I was guiding my sister Hepzibah when we played together, and explaining the music to my accompanists, and so, as it were, teaching. And clearly the conductor is a guide, is a teacher.

There is a great psychological difference between the violinist, who depends entirely upon himself for the sound he makes, and the conductor or the teacher, who must coax it out of the orchestra or the student. It is an entirely different achievement, sometimes frustrating, sometimes deeply rewarding. Both in their way complement each other and when one has brought a group of musicians so far as to give a remarkable performance of an important work, it is proof of one's ability to communicate without antagonizing, because so much is so often lost by inhibiting, by discouraging.

The act of teaching should be a pointing of the way, but even more of releasing energies which already, from the very beginning, want to go that way. For every musician, even playing in the last stand of the orchestra, is one who began his life with a vision of musical expression.

The teacher must not be too arrogant and proud. One of his chief functions is to avoid doing harm. I would say that at least nine out of ten, and probably ninety-nine out of a hundred, teachers do harm; they are not aware, perhaps in their vanity and their blindness, of the damage they are doing. If a teacher can avoid this negative achievement, if he avoids doing any harm even if he does not do any good, he is already a pretty good teacher.

I have already mentioned that if a violinist plays out of tune it is not that he cannot hear. Perhaps he doesn't hear because he cannot be different, cannot alter because of a physical or technical defect. It is not that he wouldn't like to hear, but that he simply cannot play in tune.

A teacher must always look for the cause behind a disability and attempt to correct the original root reason – to

136

give the student a real groundwork. It is no use saying: 'Your rhythm is bad'. A good teacher studies the pupil to see how he walks, whether he can dance, whether he understands what rhythm is all about. Is rhythm for him some vague, intellectual concept, or does it really go into his toes, his legs and eventually his fingers?

And the student must feel, each time he has seen his teacher, that he has gained a new insight, that a further step has been achieved, or that something has been put right. Mistakes are only means of opening our eyes to the correction, and each mistake makes us more aware, stronger, clearer and better informed. Mistakes are not to be merely criticized as mistakes. Any fool can hear a scratch or an uneven, out-of-tune note on the violin. That is hardly worth mentioning. What is obvious, and obvious to the student too, does not have to be stressed. It is what the student cannot explain and cannot correct that is the teacher's responsibility.

The teacher should remember that progress never proceeds along a straight path in an unwavering direction. It is rather a zig-zag course; we often learn more when we fall back than when we forge ahead. To progress, we must have vision, patience and perseverance.

It is also very rewarding to be able to give and to receive, or at least to note with happy thankfulness the satisfaction that grows in the student. And it is nice, as one ages, to help the young and to feel that in this way continuity of achievement, continuity of progress, is ensured. There is nothing that keeps one young as effectively as the young themselves. Their buoyancy, their hope and faith, their trust – these are the qualities with which we must surround ourselves as we get older.

I have met people who have made a great success of their lives by knowing when to give up the violin; but it is sad that so often they haven't even kept it up for their own pleasure. And this is simply because they were badly taught.

There have, of course, been great teachers. But today we require good, ordinary violin teachers in abundance, and those able to teach a class. The Japanese, Suzuki, was perhaps the first to evolve a method of teaching the violin in class. His ambition, as he disarmingly told me, is to create a generation of amateurs, and he is so right. The amateur – literally one who loves – is the person who adores his work; and no art, and no achievement in society, can flourish unless it is based on thousands of people who are dedicated amateurs – on people who love to paint, to build, to cook, to play the violin.

Suzuki was quick to realize that there are different forms of learning, and that the earliest, the child's grasping of what he calls 'the mother tongue', is learnt by example and imitation. This happens almost from the moment a child is born, and indeed Suzuki puts violins into the hands of children of three, but not before he has trained a parent or both parents in the rudiments of the art, so that they may supervise and guide the child. This is a very Japanese approach – there, parents still guide their children, unlike the United States where children tend to guide their parents!

This method has been adapted to Western use where, after all, we have a different mentality, a more emancipated youth, and a need for a wider variety of repertoire (the Suzuki repertoire, for example, largely ignores contemporary forms). This adaptation has been undertaken by Paul Rowland at the University of Detroit, who has prepared a series of films, books and compositions, written by some of the most talented young composers in the United States, for each stage and grade of the method. I believe that here lies a very fine source of material for use in our schools.

I feel that my own contribution is one of clarifying the stages and requirements of violin technique (see pp. 40-79) and of applying the same clarification and analysis to the requirements of interpretation (see pp. 103-6).

Ten
Lessons at the Yehudi Menuhin School

This chapter is a transcription from tape of a teaching session that took place at the Menuhin school at Stoke d'Abernon, in Surrey, with the author and three of his young pupils. It is included here since it illustrates very vividly Menuhin's approach to the teaching of the violin; which perhaps may be said to be a total commitment to the needs of his pupils – not only from the viewpoint of technique, vital and immeasurably demanding though this is. Yet Menuhin's method goes far beyond the point of purely technical excellence, which the reader of this book will certainly appreciate.

The first lesson began, quite spontaneously, from the moment a small boy took his violin from its case and began warming up with a fragment from Mozart.*

Lesson one

The student is a young boy.
Student: (Violin).†

Mozart Rondo

YM: All right, you can keep that, it's the recognized
        traditional fingering where they never use the
        second position, but if you like to slide up and

*The lessons were transcribed by Eric Fenby.
† The words (Violin) or (Vocal) indicate playing or humming.

change position from the B to the C on the first finger (vocal) then you don't have any real shift at all, you see?

YM: (Violin).

Student: But surely it's more likely to get a little more out of tune if you do it that way?

YM: It's not more likely to go out of tune if your fingers are accustomed to the second position. It's inclined to be less trouble, and less fuss, and less break, because you just move a half tone. Anyway, you try that. Very often in a passage like this – a fast passage – I'd rather move two half tones unobtrusively than two whole tones in one jump. One jump, unless you are very deft, may give a little bump, shall we say. All right, try the Mendelssohn.

Student: (Violin: plays to 4 bars after B .) See opposite.

YM: A few things – some technical, some musical. Now, the technical thing is you're bent, crouched over the violin. You know that: I've told you – in fact everyone has told you.

Student: Yes, yes.

YM: Yes, how are we going to get out of it? Can you play the beginning with the feeling that you have just come out into the fresh air and that you are just so happy, after being in a room where there has been a lot of smoke, and you are so happy to be able to fill your lungs with air.

Just – (sounds of breathing) – just – can you breathe in and out (sounds of breathing)? Can you

Mendelssohn's Violin Concerto, Op. 64

do that with your hands at a certain playing level?
No, look at it. It's not quite right. Just move round
like that from one side to the other – what's this
hand doing? This is the violin hand. It should

141

also be balanced and float in the air, and can you coordinate the two so that they look natural? In the same direction – like te-ta, te-ta, te-ta – as if they are waving.

You've seen those wonderful plants that grow under the water; you know how softly they move in the currents under the water. You've seen them in gold fish bowls. This movement can look like those lovely weeds, or whatever they call them, waving in the water.

And now can you produce the wave by a gentle going from one side, the feet slightly far apart – that's right! Now push yourself from one group of toes to the other, but not as one piece, you see. They don't go like that as one piece. The wave carries it from the toes to the head, and keep that in the playing position. That's nice! Can you get yourself looking approximately here (at eye level) and filling yourself with air as you do that?

If you continue the old way you will grow up crooked. You still haven't grown your full height; if anything is unbalanced at this stage then it will get worse. That's the only danger of learning the violin young. I don't want that. The way to test posture is to hang either from the head or the feet and then you know that the weight carries you in a straight line.

All right. Try again. Just a slight wave with the feet like that, neither so far apart that one cannot shift weight easily from one foot to the other, nor so near as to lose stability.

Try to go from the beginning as if you were drawing circles on the floor with each hand, one after the other, not both together – separately – like that. Draw circles with both hands. That's it. Now gradually keep that going – keep that going and now draw circles against the ceiling with both hands. Yes, but in the right playing position with

142

Plate 8. Low right arm – the correct bowing position
Plate 9. To tip
Plate 10. High right arm – a bowing position of which I disapprove for the viola

↑ 8

↑ 9

10

↑ 11

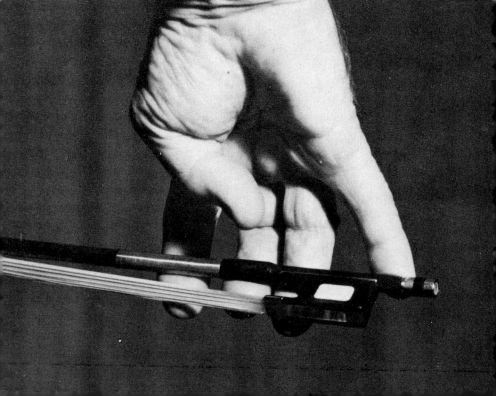

the other one still as if you were drawing on the
floor. That's right – and this draws on the ceiling.
That's right. The left hand draws on the ceiling
and the right hand draws on the table.

Now breathe – in, out, in, out, fast and slow. Do
it fast (sounds of breathing). Fill your mouth,
which is not the way you're going to do it, but just
to fill your lungs – that's right. And when you've
done that three times do it slowly. One, two – in,
out. Close your mouth. That's right. All right. Now,
that will happen instantaneously. You won't see
the results yet, but gradually you will find that you
are beginning the Mendelssohn concerto with that
feeling of floating, because it is a floating beginning,
although it is agitated, but it is agitated in a kind of
breezy way (vocal: sings opening phrase).

If you're crouched over your violin it's no
good because you crush whatever wants to fly; you
don't want to pin it down. Playing the violin is a
kind of flying; you want it to take off, to take wing.
So play it with that feeling if you can. It won't
happen immediately. Try that now.

Student: (Violin.)

YM: That's better. But you notice – each down-bow,
        te-da, te-da – as if you were paying obeisance to
        some invisible deity. Try and replace your Japanese
        salutation. You know, the Japanese do that when-
        ever they meet somebody, even if it's in the middle
        of the street and against the traffic. It's a wonderful
        way for pedestrians to behave; but you do that as

Plate 11. Defying gravity – the 'parlour trick'   143
Plate 12. How the 'parlour trick' is accomplished

a matter of course each time you take a down-bow!
Just play a few Bs down-bow.

Student: (Violin Bs.)

YM: That's better.

Student: (More violin Bs.)

YM: Ah, you saw it happen there. Exactly. Avoid that.

Student: (Violin: repeats Bs.)

YM: Yes, that's right. No – it was just coming again. Keep your head straight, like that. And use the whole bow and rather exaggerate the motion.

Student: (Violin: repeats Bs.)

YM: That's much better. And when you take the up-bow almost go that way, but don't dip into the down-bow. Let your head go almost away from your hands as it comes up in the up-bow. Don't go to meet it. That's something that's supposed to be the remains – I spoke the other day to some of you – it's supposed to be the remains of fear – the fear an infant has of falling, so it raises its right arm to protect itself and to shelter the head. We must grow out of that fear. Try again.

Student: (Violin: repeats Bs.)

YM: That's much better. And in the up-bow let the head sort of lead the bow.

Student: I'm going to have to make a mental effort to do that.

YM: You're going to have to make a mental effort, but later on the good thing about a good habit is that it's actually much easier than a bad habit. The mental effort, however, is required to see it clearly and to develop the sense of enjoyment and pleasure and ease that comes with the good habit. The good habit is really much simpler than the bad habit; but the bad habit has a hold on you because you fear, not the loss of a bad habit, but the absence of a good habit to replace it. So first, as you say, you have to have a mental effort, to have a clear picture. Once the mind knows exactly what it wants the body will follow. You should have a clear idea of this and when you've done it a few times rightly, just go on.

Student: (Violin.)

YM: That's right. Now, did you see? Were you there this morning? Were you in class?

Student: I was there.

YM: You were? Sorry, I should have noticed you. . . . Now, remember, you start off without any spring. It's the spring we were discussing this morning.

Student: (Violin.)

YM: No, don't dig. Do it on a B. Three or four in a row.

Student: (Violin: repeats Bs.)

YM: Now, are you doing it this way each time? The third finger on the bow should pull – should overlap the stick so that it has a little purchase on the outside of the stick, and the first finger should press the stick and both fingers should go slightly, very slightly, apart to get the better pressure, whilst the thumb opposes the clockwise roll of the bow.

Student: (Violin: repeats Bs.)

YM: Don't lean on the violin.

Student: (Violin: repeats Bs moving into opening bars of concerto.)

YM: And can you combine that with your swing? That's right (vocal). Now. Again (vocal). Start off with your engine running already. Good. Mind – it's beginning to dip again. You see what I mean? That's fine. And the whole of your playing should be on this level of floating and being carried away on the feeling of lift and lightness so that you don't get this dip.

Right. You will, I hope, remember this and work at it. Look at yourself in the mirror, and each time you can't see yourself you know that your head and body are bent forward. Right. Now go ahead. And you see how much nicer this is because

it is smooth. It was smooth because you had the
'give' in there from the pressure and from the float.
Now do you want to do where the triplets come?

Begin again, begin again. It's so nice. It's better
now. It's not as nice as it will be. No dips. Just feel
that everything is floating, and things don't float
vertically; they float horizontally. You see? And
the whole thing must do that.

Student: (Violin: opening of concerto as far as B.)

YM: Try again – without the dip. Look up at the ceiling.

Student: (Violin: from A.)

YM: Did you see the Japanese girl last night with the
Bach A minor? Well, she had an extraordinary
habit of giving her head a shake each time she
went down-bow and up-bow. It didn't add to the
down-bow and up-bow but it had this – if you only
looked, you thought she had this tremendous
attack; if you listened, the attack was in the head
only.

Student: (Violin.)

YM: Now, can you take a few intermediate strokes?
You start off and before you get to the end of the
stroke you should already be going the other way.

Student: (Violin: octaves again.)

YM: That's right. Just a little more slowly. And when
you take a down-bow don't land like that on the

string as if the arm were a dead weight, but land less vertically.

Student: (Violin: octaves again.)

YM: You see you are holding the bow with the fingers all stiff. It creates great tension in the whole arm and prevents you doing anything subtle.

Student: (Violin.)

Student: Can I just say something?

YM: Please.

Student: What does it really matter if you can do it another way, say stiff?

YM: It doesn't, if you can bring it off; but it matters very much because you lay up trouble for yourself. Each time you use a muscle unnecessarily – each time you use more than the one you need and don't let the others rest, you're building up residual tension whereby the muscles get used to remaining in a state of high tension to no purpose. Then instead of being able to control the motion, you find that you are always having to deal with other muscles that are intruding on the motion and you will never be able to get a pure, clean, correct motion. It's like having a lot of impurities in a substance like gold or water. If you hold the bow in a tight way, the fact that you are continuously depending on the thumb and the fingers for the grip, and they can't leave go because there's no balance and flexibility, no continuous adjustment of the fingers to each other, means that they have

147

got to hold on in this tight way as you might hold on to a club. Thus you are imposing a continuous strain. Now nothing in life is made to remain always in one state of tension.

If you keep up tension longer than necessary you are in for trouble. In fact I don't know whether the tension begins because the body is not moving sympathetically or because the fingers, which are the end of our limbs, are holding on too stiffly. It's a combination of both, for as soon as we get a balanced, flexible and sturdy hold in the fingers, it helps the rest of the body to relax. We must never forget that the fingers are the last things we have there – the extremities. So that whatever motion we have always starts from the earth: it always starts from the earth because that's the point upon which we stand. That's the resistance we have. It starts from the earth and travels through the body to the fingers. If the fingers start with a tension which isn't controlled by the flow, the wave flow of energy through the body, then you are dealing with the violin as if you had at the end of your arm, not hand and fingers, but a crowbar.

You couldn't do much with a crowbar and that's the reason why you must always work for the most elegant, the most economical, the most effective motion (violin). This body-supporting motion is something you must not indulge in and exaggerate, but as soon as you have achieved a balance and a freedom of motion you don't even have to show it. It's there. It's like something which is free to move. The head is balanced on the spine. One does not have to shake it to prove that it's loose. It's there – it's loose. When the body moves, it has to adjust. In the same way, if you play well, you don't have to move very much.

Good. Go ahead with it. I have spoken enough about this for you to think about.

Mendelssohn concerto, continued

As you were carried away and played so beautifully – nice sound, nice vibrato – you got more and more into the old position. You must guard against it yourself and remind yourself. Don't let one mistake pass: when you practise you will be continually correcting yourself, and gradually it will be a pleasure.

Student: (Violin.)

YM: That was a bit awkward!

It's because your fingers are inclined to be too low on the finger-board, so that each time you have to have a shift it's a major affair. I'll show you so that you can see what I mean. This is squashed (violin) and it's difficult to get up. If you are stopped by the violin, you are stopped by the fact that the elbow is here, too low. You see, you can hardly get anywhere. That's why I want you to have this space (violin). Let your shoulder fall back so that you make all possible space available (violin).

Let us see how you go from a low position to a high position: how you prepare it. Yes. Now can you hold the fingers that high, and just before the shift let the shoulder fall back? The thumb should never be directly below the neck nor too far over, just somewhere on the other side of the middle.

Student: (Violin.)

YM: Yes, only why were these fingers so close together? And how would you shift back from a very high position?

Student: (Violin.)

YM: It's not very good. I'll show you if you watch. The little release of falling slightly forward with the shoulder and then beginning back perhaps before

150

the hand. That's better than it was, but it still isn't perfect because the violin is too low.

Student: (Violin.)

YM: Lift the violin as you go down. But keep in contact with the string all the time.

Student: (Violin.)

YM: Slowly. As you go down lift the violin to that point. Gradually. That's better. That's it.

Student: (Violin.)

YM: That's it. Without the whole body leaning forward.

Student: (Violin.)

YM: That's better. But don't fall on the last note. Well, I think I've tortured you enough!

Student: Thank you very much indeed.

Lesson two

A second student now joined Yehudi Menuhin, a girl in her teens. She played Hindemith's Sonata for Solo Violin, Op. 31, No. 1.

fur Liceo Amar

SONATE

VIOLINE

I

Paul Hindemith, Op.31, No.1

Sehr lebhafte Achtel

Hindemith's Sonata for Solo Violin, Op. 31, No. 1

YM: Wouldn't it be easier with the fourth finger on the
          G sharp and first on the B?

Student: (Violin.) (See bar 7)

YM: Good. That's good.

Student: (Violin.)

YM: Look, don't try to play too much as if it were a
          concert performance because I don't want you to
          do anything that would spoil your good form.

Student: (Violin.)

YM: Don't work too hard; loosen after every effort.
          Another good thing for trills and for the left hand
          is to release between each note as if you had a
          harmonic between each note. That is very useful
          because that prevents the tension from continuing
          through two notes, let alone eight.

          Let's try another movement; which one would
          you prefer?

Student: The third.

YM: All right.

Student: (Violin.)

III

153

Hindemith sonata, continued

YM: This movement has – actually it's very difficult to play and you haven't seen it in a long time, but it has tremendous humour (vocal). It has great wit and bite.

It's very interesting. You see, you can look at music in various ways. You can look at it pictorially, even. I love to look at Bach manuscripts pictorially, because you *see* – he drew his five lines and you see the flow of the music: he never hesitated for a moment. It's a wonderful, strong flow. But here –

look at the opening bars of this third movement.
This is the humorous part:

and then you have the cantabile (vocal):

And the fact that the quavers become triplets and
finally semi-quavers is a progression. And you
often find, like my thinking, music proceeds by
opposites. We think only in opposites, or we go
crab-wise . . . at least I do. Immediately I visualize
one thing I ask myself, now what is its opposite?
It's a perverse way of thinking and I think many
people are perverse. You see the sun, this beautiful
weather. But what is it like now at the South Pole –
dark and dismal? Or what if it rains, what if we
have a cloud-burst? And the same thing – any kind
of continuity progresses both according to one
way of sameness and the other of contrast. This:

would be a mystery contrasted with the obviousness of:

Hindemith loved sport and played tennis – no one would have mistaken him for a composer if one had met him on the street. Above all – he was terribly clear. He tried to reduce everything to understandable equations and method. You use his book here at the school – a book of rhythms, but he also wrote a book on harmony in which he tried to produce a system which would do equally for classical and contemporary harmonies. He established an order of intervals, an order of increasing dissonance and decreasing stability in which the fifth is more important than the third, and third more important than the second, the major second than the minor second; he then decided that no matter what chord you analysed, wherever you discovered a perfect fifth, the lower note of that fifth was the *fundamental*, which is a very ingenious way of getting around the dissonances. If he wrote a major third or a minor one, or a second, I think he was very aware of their degree of dissonance and their degree of importance. I am sure that he felt right through this fifth bar that the C is the important note harmonically, because it is the root of the major third which is more important in his mind than the diminished fifth. This impression is accentuated because the highest and lowest notes of bar 4 are the leading notes B.

And then another contrast is rise and fall. For instance, here you have fall, here you have rise. The first two bars are fall, the second two bars are rise. That's what I call a pictorial view of the music and you will find that the contrasts occur in fall and rise, in short and long, in laughing and singing, in piano and forte, in obviousness and in mystery – and these are contrasts you must look out for, especially when you are dealing with a composition which is unlike a classical work. To make this musically alive you have to look at it in all these aspects, and then see patterns and see shapes and see contrasts in terms of texture, of volume, of rhythm, of harmony; and as soon as you catch these contrasts and catch the structure of the piece, as you can here, then you understand it. Even though his music can be so intricate and complicated, it has absolute clarity in his mind. I know, too, that he wrote visually. He could compose a piece with any number of people in the room making any amount of noise and he told me that he once composed a double canon on a train!

He knew where he wanted a consonance, where he wanted a dissonance and when you see the first pianissimo, well it means something – it means well here's a new rhythm that hasn't been heard before, and it's the beginning of a succession where this rhythm is going to appear. The succession can rise from here to the high note, can go down and up again. It's actually extremely obvious music in its own way, simply because of the clarity that he had, structurally, pictorially, and in every way, because he was able to impose or to resolve mysteries or things that were vague – he hated anything that wasn't absolutely clear, and in fact he brought an extraordinary penetration of insight into everything. And you see here in the fourth movement he doesn't indicate a mood of expression, say, of humour or sadness but gives specific instructions to be played softly and delicately and with quietly flowing quavers. And that's typical of him – he just wanted to say the essential and with no descriptive ornamentation. That is the nearest he came to giving you a clue of the feeling, but he wants it *in tempo*; because he said 'slowly', the quavers should move at equal pace. This is a lovely movement.

IV

Intermezzo, Lied. Ganz leise und zart zu spielen
Ruhig bewegte Achtel

Hindemith sonata, continued

He would, I am sure, be very clear which notes were more important and which notes were less important, not only in the vertical harmonic texture but also in the melodic one. He writes a crescendo here. There again, we have rise and fall. Obviously each time he recalls the opening bar it becomes increasingly tender. Anything rising needs energy to push it up and you have to have more aggressiveness and tension and volume to lift things, unless they're floating, unless they take off of themselves like a balloon or floating away on a current of air as in a sailplane. Otherwise, if you are rising from the ground by your own effort, it's not a tender feeling, it's a – either a feeling of great anticipation if it's inevitable, or a feeling of elation, or of strength, of gathering strength. But anything falling is either a caress or a collapse. These principles also apply to notes as they do to engineering, only engineers don't know anything about it usually! They don't build expressive buildings because they have forgotten this truth. This whole movement is actually one texture. It's all simple, the whole thing. There are no detached notes; they are all legato. It's a gentle song, and very regretful.

I think there are key feelings which lie behind most music – regretful, fearful, aggressive, dominant, tender, volcanic – anything. You can use all kinds of words. But in this case it is the nostalgic and regretful.

Student: Especially the following thirds (violin).

YM: Following thirds, exactly. Repeated memories (violin).

Student: Yes.

YM: As I have said, a repeated memory is a nostalgic thing (vocal). Three times he repeats it, each time more softly:

And the fact that he doesn't put this in an even rhythm (vocal) gives you a little catch, the two

V

Hindemith sonata, continued

greater pauses a sort of sigh (vocal). The last is putting it to sleep. If you can see things that way it helps you give it shape, meaning; and also to convey it to the public, because the public doesn't know this, and if they are to judge merely by the notes you are playing without any conception behind them, they won't get the message.

Student: Would you say that it's a movement entirely in contrast to the last movement which is a block . . . ?

YM: Yes, it's a block of speed; that's all it is and it's like a whirlwind. It's like Chopin's 'Funeral March' Sonata that has that extraordinary whirlwind last movement. It sounds like leaves falling in autumn, just whirling. And this is a little bit the same idea; it just disappears – except, of course, for the crescendo, which is the end of the whole sonata: You're perfectly right about the shapes. That's where he was sometimes a little too obvious.

Student: Do you think he was influenced by Bach?

YM: I am sure, especially by the C Major Sonata. I think anybody who has written solo sonatas for violin has been influenced by Bach's solo sonatas. Well, thank you for giving me the opportunity of looking at this fine sonata.

Lesson three

Yehudi Menuhin's third pupil was a boy, who chose the Adagio of the G Minor Solo Violin Sonata of Bach.

Student: (Violin.)

YM: Now let's start immediately with this. This is an introduction like the chromatic fantasy and fugue. It is a kind of fantasy, and this is the first statement. When you present it, when you play it, you must give it the importance of a portal, as if you're moving into a great temple – there it stands, it's a statement. And I would hold on – it's a general rule with Bach – I would hold on to the resolution of the

163

SONATA No. 1

interval with both notes, long enough to hear the resolution of the harmony. I apply this principle in the fugues as well, for instance in the C major fugue with the minims that accompany the theme, the minims of chromatic descent. I play them and crotchets plus at least a semi-quaver. The semi-quaver is long enough to hold over the change of note and harmony so that the hearer hears the resolution or the dissonance as the case may be. So I hold the C with the F sharp just long enough so that the ear hears the two together.

Then begin again. You see, the beginning didn't have any grandeur.

Student: (Violin.)

YM: Good! You know that this is very important because very often you find the seed of the next movement in the first one:
(Violin.)

When you come to this point you want to plant it in the public's – the listener's memory. So you play it importantly enough for them to carry it over and find a natural evolution when it becomes in fact the fugal theme:
(Violin.)

Look at yourself in the mirror. In fact you and a few others should ask Mr Norris if you can play for the video tape. It'll do you a little good. Naturally, you can judge from the mirror too, but it's not the same thing because you don't move freely. You're fixed on your own image in the mirror which isn't good. But the video tape will take you from a distance and then you'll be rather disappointed when you see yourself at first, and you will have to – you will want to correct it.

Student: (Violin.)

YM: Why do you do that on a D string? That's one of the things I always want to say about playing Bach, and that is that the most important thing is the voice leading. If you are on the D string, from where is the B flat going to come? Are you going back on the A string for that?

Student: Yes.

YM: Well, the E flat and B flat belong together. They should be on the same string. If you go on the D string it's really a violinistic effect which is quite out of place in Bach. It's much better, as a general rule, to remain in low positions. I'm sure Bach wrote his music with a definite fingering in mind. He couldn't have written the complicated chords which can only be done one way unless he had that one way in mind when he was composing. I'm sure he wrote with the fingering in mind, and although once or twice I have let myself be tempted by a romantic fingering, you have to do it extremely discreetly. But here I think it's out of place.

Do you know why there is an open A too? Because if you take the fourth finger on the A you have the first finger on the B flat. And if the two

strings sound together you will have a wrong
interval. So I wouldn't be shy about open strings.
They can be made to sound beautiful, of course –
but I would use the open A there.

Part Two

The Viola
by William Primrose

Eleven
The Viola

An instrument in its own right

A witty Frenchman once remarked: '*Ce qui est trop bête pour être chanté, on le danse.*' Similarly, he who is too beastly on the violin, throw him a viola. At least that was the attitude towards violinists and the viola from the distant past until Lionel Tertis emerged and restored the instrument to what he believed, and what I and others also believe, was its rightful position. Hellmuth Christian Wolff, in the preface to his edition of the *Telemann Concerto in G Major for Viola* (Bärenreiter, 1968), reminds us that in the seventeenth century the viola was held in much higher regard than in the years to follow. It is instructive to read that:

The viola da braccia was introduced into the orchestra in the 17th century as a kind of 'filling-up' instrument. At first it was used as a subordinate instrument to support the second violins or the bass (in the higher octave), but was already also given its own part in Venice or appeared doubled (with two obbligato parts) in the opera orchestra (cf. my book *Die venezianische Oper in der zweiten Hälfte des 17. Jahrhunderts*, Berlin 1937. Supplement No. 6, 9, 10, 18 and so on). In baroque opera it was preferred to use the viola for special purposes; thus Antonio Draghi prescribed two concertante violas for the Ritornello of his opera *Creso* (Vienna 1678 III, 19) and also a complete viola quintet for the accompaniment of an aria in the same opera (II, 14). Two concertante violas enjoyed particular popularity in the Lament-Arias of the Venetian opera, for instance in *Il Candaule* (1679) by Pietro Andrea Ziani or in *Onorio in Roma* (1692) by Carlo Francesco Pollaroli (these arias are mentioned in the appendix Nos. 46 and 65 in my book on the Venetian opera). With the development of the orchestra to string quartet ensemble the viola parts were again reduced to one, to which, however, increased attention was

171

given. This is already evident in the Sinfonia to the opera *Messalina* (Venice 1680) by Carlo Pallavicini (mentioned in appendix No. 67 of my *Venetian Opera*), then to a larger extent in the concertos of the early 18th century (cf. Arnold Schering, *Geschichte des Instrumentalkonzerts*, Leipzig 1927, p. 18). As a solo concertante instrument the viola da braccia also made its first appearance in opera, for instance in a sonata of the opera *Le promesse degli Dei* (Vienna 1697) by F. T. Richter, side by side with the concertante violin, violino piccolo and bass viola, as well as three flutes and string orchestra. In the opera *Almira* (Hamburg 1704) by G. Fr. Handel and further in the opera *Diana* (Hamburg 1712) by Reinhard Keiser the viola is used for the solo accompaniment of an aria. Reinhard Keiser in the opera *Octavia* (Hamburg 1705) characterized several songs of Nero by concertante viola accompaniment, and Christoph Graupner treated the arias of the love-sick Antiochus similarly in *Antiochus und Stratonica* (Hamburg 1708). Telemann is one of those composers who brought to Germany the Italian concert form and there developed it independently. The viola concerto by Telemann was probably written – as was a large part of his 170 instrumental concertos – for the 'weekly great concertos in the "Frauenstein" ' at Frankfurt on Main which he himself directed. The fact that Torelli and the church sonata were used as models is recognizable from the four-movement structure. As far as details are concerned, however, the concerto bears in full the stamp of Telemann's personal artistry, his gay and pleasant amiability, his understanding of the instrument in question and its tonal character. Thus the various positions of the viola are skilfully turned to account (leaps and low register in the 1st movement; high register in the 2nd movement, etc.). Sudden harmonic turns (as in the 1st movement, bar 55, 3rd movement, bars 25/26) are part of Telemann's individual style, as is the occasional silencing of the basso continuo (in the 2nd and 3rd movements). The 4th movement has the character of a merry dance, such as a 'Bourrée'. Telemann prefers to place similar movements at the end of his solo concertos, as for example in the violin concerto in A minor (which was the Overture to the opera *Emma und Eginhard*, Hamburg 1728; cf. my new edition in the series *Hortus Musicus* No. 32, published by Bärenreiter).

As a concertante solo instrument Telemann further used the viola in a Concert Overture and in addition in a concerto for two violettas and string orchestra. These concertos must not be compared with J. S. Bach's 6th Brandenburg Concerto (for two solo violas, Cöthen 1721). Telemann's style is an entirely different one; in contrast to the heavy – often opaque – polyphony of

Bach, Telemann paid stronger regard to the tone, the clarity and the pure prominence of the solo instrument.

However, this is no place to enter further into the history of the viola and viola playing. Books of reference and research abound and the curious will learn most of what they wish to know from them, much more than I can offer here considering the limitations and purposes of the following chapter. The fact remains, nevertheless, that after its moment of glory, to which Wolff refers, the viola was neglected by players and composers alike. Which neglect came first poses a question that is in 'the hen or the egg' category. It is difficult to say. The reasons are more readily discerned. Composers, I fancy, did not care to write for an instrument that was so badly served by those who played it. And players did not wish to be associated with one, at once doleful in sound and lacking in repertoire. The violins, on the other hand, and the violinists coruscated in a magnitude of brilliance and sweetness, whilst the violists dwelt in the sombre shadows. When Tertis arrived this unfortunate state of affairs began to change and the viola began to be established as a very definite entity with a character and a place of its own. No man, the poet tells us, is an island unto himself, and while one admits that in the archipelago of strings no one instrument is an island unto itself, the autonomy of each must be clearly defined and recognized, the better that the whole may prosper. That in some cases this autonomy is not properly appreciated is disclosed by the number of violinists today who appear to believe that all they have to do is to possess themselves of a viola, and play away on it to their heart's content and my distress, not realizing for a moment that all that is happening is that they are performing on what I am prompted to call the 'big-fiddle', denying it (the viola, that is) its uniqueness, its quiddity. That I do not attribute this unfortunate practice to my admirable and respected friend Mr Menuhin will become manifest in the course of the remarks and observations he has requested me to contribute to his book. There are, too, some others like him who give to the viola the essence and tang that characterize it and lend it separateness from the other strings. I would suggest, however, that unless a violinist has addressed himself to the proper study of the viola, his deft performance is fortuitous. I have absolutely no objection to this at any time. All that interests me is the consequent sound that should distinguish it at once. These happy few I shall continue to refer to as violinists, while the 'criminals' of the other category, those who perform their antics on the 'big-fiddle', I shall refer to, with proper distaste I am persuaded, as mere 'fiddlers'!

Tertis in England, and Maurice Vieux in France, laid down certain principles of viola playing that have established the two countries as a sort of *fons et origo* of viola playing, but in the early days of their respective careers they were as voices crying in a wilderness of unawareness. I never met or knew Vieux, but I knew Lionel Tertis very well, and I am fully aware that he was alert to the fact that he was not going to get anywhere in his crusade without storming and battering the citadel of apathy which dismissed violists and the instrument to the deepest dungeon of indifference and low esteem. And storm and battle he did. It was a battle of heroic proportions, and in battle he was supreme. For those of us who followed in his train our task was rendered all the more easy and recognition was no longer withheld. He was the first, to my knowledge, who insisted on the uniqueness of the viola, its quiddity as I have already expressed it. Tertis defined the distinct personality of the instrument, and to suggest that performance on it was no more than playing the violin a fifth down in pitch was to commit the sin of sins and evoke his wrath both swift and devastating. May I add that mine is similarly evoked? The two great distinctions between violin and viola playing lie in the proper use of fingering and bowing, two categories I shall deal with in detail.

Bowing

To finger the viola as if it were the analogue of the violin is

Plate 13–16. A well-tried method of positioning. (In the two standing pictures, my right leg is advanced instead of the left; this is, of course, because I am, for the moment, holding the viola with my right hand. And in the final picture I am looking slightly to the left . . .)

↑ 13

↑ 14

15

16

18

to do the very thing that brought the former into such ill repute. Its tonal recalcitrance is abetted, and its peculiar sonority is muted. Thus, no doubt, did it come to be regarded as the dull dog of the string family. The bow technique is much more circumscribed. By that I mean that there exist many theories of violin bow technique, explicitly laid down by their protagonists, and largely successful in the matter of tone production. This latitude is possible, I have no doubt, because of the greater responsiveness of the violin. But such is not the case when we come to play the viola. We are constantly dealing with problems of sonority and tractability. Consequently we violists are more restricted in our methods and constrained to greater care in matters of tone production. Those violinists whom I have heard to good effect on the viola have, fortuituously, as suggested elsewhere, employed a bowing technique in their violin playing which admirably suited the viola.

A 'fiddler', once asked just how much difference he found when he presumed to play the viola, replied that all he had to do was to press harder! An ignorant and frivolous reply I am apt to think. No! The words 'pressure' and 'viola' are immiscible. Has the reader observed that in French editions of music, especially *études*, what is called an *Explication des Signes* is included? In that table he will see ⊓ referred to as *tirez*, and ∨ as *poussez*. To pull and push the bow in playing viola is of the essence. To press leads to well-deserved disaster. I have never observed Mr Menuhin play the viola, but last time I heard him, in an almost too moving performance of the Elgar violin concerto, he was drawing the tone from his violin in a fashion that boded no ill for its application to the lower pitched instrument. Those of us who studied with Eugène Ysaye were thus taught to bow and, by the way, he was a rare violinist performer on the viola. Not a 'fiddler', mark you. Moreover, the matter of crossing from one string to another was awarded the closest attention. We were adjured to follow the arc of the bridge, which can only be achieved by the arm being lower than the stick itself, exerting a pulling motion

Plate 17. An incorrect hold – I am tightening my neck muscles to look at my left hand . . . to see if it is still there?

Plate 18. An exercise in contortion – here my left shoulder is dangerously out of position (see plates 8 and 9).* Ysaye convinced us that, with the arm on a higher plane than the stick, pressure and pushing will result, and the bow will progress in a series of bumps from string to string, somewhat like a ball rolling down a flight of steps (see plate 10). No! and, again, no! to pressure or anything like it. There are, of course, colleagues who disagree, and disfavour the low arm and the 'pull-push' system. There are some, surrendering to the mistaken assumption that, because of its construction (the upper portion of the bow being weaker than the lower), they must resort to pressure to compensate. At the risk of being regarded as 'rude and scant of courtesy' I am constrained to declare: 'Incompetent nonsense!' I have made a career and gained a not too unenviable reputation as a tone-spinner proving the fallacy of 'press' and the speciousness of 'high arm'. A point that I stress in teaching is the grip on the stick involving the thumb and the second finger, although this is not unique to the viola. But, a weakness in this regard, like so many other weaknesses, will be more rapidly exposed on the viola than the violin. I emphasize the importance of a firm and *supple* grip, and if a player be derelict in this duty I do not have to look to be aware of it. I can readily tell by the resulting sound. A careless, loose grip will produce a tone that is fuzzy and lacking in body. Also I have no difficulty in snatching the bow from the startled and bewildered student, and have discovered that such Draconian method creates a lasting impression on the transgressor!

I would like to point out, at this juncture, that when I put my bow in the viola case at the end of a performance or study period, I like to imagine that I am, in a sense, detaching one-third of my arm in so doing, and conversely, when I resume playing, I am reuniting that third with the lower and upper arm which constitute the other two-thirds. Now these two-thirds are joined at the elbow and no amount of ordinary pulling and tugging is likely to separate one from the other. They are firmly united and yet, unless the joint is diseased, ankylosed for example, the two sections enjoy perfect free-

*Plates 8, 9 and 10 are opposite page 142.

dom of movement in relation to one another. This type of relationship should prevail between the thumb and second finger and the detachable part of the arm we call the bow, the thumb and second finger forming another elbow, so to speak, with the frog.

The position of the fingers on the stick is, as I believe from much experience, of vast importance. The position should approximate to that adopted by a fine cellist, with the fingers encircling the stick much more amply than is common practice on the violin. To impress my students with the great importance of this I am wont to perform what at first may appear to be a frivolous 'parlour trick', and it does indeed create a marked impression and a look of unbelief. This 'parlour trick' (see plates 11 and 12), with which I confound the incredulous, enables me to hold the bow with the fingers alone *with no aid from the thumb*, and in any position, any angle. That is to say, with the point towards the roof, towards the floor, and any of the numerous angles in between. (The viola is not involved in these manoeuvres. Leave it in the case!) However, on further inspection the student readily perceives the major part the sensitive finger pads play in cradling the stick, so to speak, and the equally important part demanded of the fourth finger as a counterbalance to the point.

Fingering

I come now to what I am persuaded is the other important difference between performance on the violin and the viola. I have already indicated that to finger the viola like a violin is a cardinal error, and one that lends to the instrument the opaqueness that all too often characterizes it in the hands of the incompetent, the unimaginative or the unenterprising. In fact I came to the conclusion a long time ago that principles of fingering that applied to the violin were simply ineffective on the larger instrument. Open strings performed freely on the violin often produce a jarring effect on the listener. *Per contra*, on the viola the open strings, as it is said of a

177

woman's hair, are its glory. That and the liberal use of natural harmonics add colour and variety that are denied by the use of conventional violin fingerings. The use of 'bariolage' is another thing I revert to frequently – that is, I cross and recross strings in order to obtain a sound more open and varied than one would dare risk on the violin. In resorting to this greater use of open strings and string crossings I also avoid passing through positional shifts as a violinist would do just to shun such specious solecisms. My fingerings in works I have edited are, I freely admit, unorthodox but always based on a reason, and one that has gone through the test of public performance as well as cogitation in the practice room, and I find it disconcerting when my unorthodoxies are erased by other teachers, and a more *respectable* fingering substituted without thought having been given to the reason behind the unorthodoxies.

An hilarious example of that sort of thing occurred some years ago in connection with my edition of the Campagnoli *Études*. I had clearly pointed out in the short foreword that the complexity and apparent eccentricity of the fingerings were prompted by an effort to introduce students to a virtuoso type of fingering that would stand them in good stead, or so I was convinced, in a new approach to fingering in general. A student enlisted in my class had been studying these works some time previously with another mentor. This person decided to amend all my fingerings and return the whole to the realms of sanity. In so doing, as I pointed out to the student, he might just as well have had the latter buy the edition by the late Sam Lifschey. Now there is nothing wrong at all with this edition by one who was the distinguished first violist of the Philadelphia Orchestra for many years. But hadn't the student's former teacher read my foreword and the very cogent reason for my apparent insanity?

A further shift from the established order (although it is a shift that is becoming more and more consecrated by custom) is the use of different fingers in broken fifths. This departure I use whenever it is possible *and* convenient. The last three words are important. I find the use of the same finger in playing broken fifths induces a certain rigidity in the left hand, which is avoided by the employment of adjacent fingers which releases the hand from its thraldom – the vice which constricts. Of course such a practice demands an agile and flexible left hand, but without such endowment one should give up any idea of becoming a string player.

To sum up: Let the violist always be conscious of the fact that he is not performing on an over-blown violin, the 'big-fiddle', and that an approach to all his problems must be, in most cases, quite different from that of the violinist; that in this day the violist is dealing with a more enlightened audience, an audience that demands that certain new requirements be met, and only a searching and inventive mind will meet them. The student must, right from the beginning, divest his mind of thinking that fingerings are chosen merely to get from one place on the finger-board to another. Indeed not. They serve a much more exalted purpose, and that purpose is to enhance the music. To be overly conscious of 'positions' is something I discourage. I rather lean towards the idea that we should think of the whole finger-board as one position, and the left hand, free and uninhibited, should never feel *obliged* to play a certain note with a certain finger. To be sure, the student must *know* the positions, and the relationship of the fingers to each other in the various territories of the finger-board; that goes without saying. But, once the knowledge is absorbed, once a complete awareness of the 'topography', so to speak, is gained, then I would advise relegating it to the unconscious mind. Something of a like nature applies to the bow. Never, never feel obliged to perform at a certain part of the bow, unless it is your wish to do so. In short, the performer must dominate the situation and should disallow the left or right hand, and their various problems, to dominate him, to bully him.

Holding and positioning

In holding the viola, as distinct from positioning it, one must eschew all thoughts that might lead one to believe that this is achieved by methods which lead to gripping the instrument

between the chin and the left shoulder with a strong resemblance to a vice, causing an intolerable cramping of all the
muscles involved, also damping out a considerable area of the
instrument, and thus acting like a mute, with the consequent
loss of sonority. No! the viola, like the violin, is held with the
left *hand*. To be sure, it has to be *rested* somewhere, and the
left shoulder is a more convenient place than, say, the breastbone – although that is just where the 'country fiddler' does
rest it, and many of them are skilful, agile and perform with
downright virtuosic abandon. Of course, he is usually playing
in one position. But here, I am persuaded, lies the clue to
the whole case: he is *resting* his fiddle on the breastbone, but
he is *holding* it with his left hand. It stands to reason that if a
player, more sophisticated and more ambitious, ascends the
finger-board, no gripping of any sort is required as the
instrument is very gently being pushed into the neck. In
descent, a very light, swift, downward pressure of the chin
(not an upward push with the shoulder) is all that is required
to prevent the instrument from slipping its moorings, *if the
player is holding it by the left hand*, just as his country cousin
does. This applies to violin playing, also, and I make no
claim that performance on the viola has no similarity to the
less noble instrument! Having got that bit of facetiae off my
chest I feel disposed to return to a more sober discussion of
our problems.

I now take up what I believe to be a bothersome one in
many cases. That is the *positioning* of the viola. And this is all
the more important when we consider the varying sizes of
instruments used by violists. As I remarked at the end of the
section on fingering, one should never be dominated by
problems, one should dominate them. But how often do we
observe a considerable asymmetry, amounting at times to
contortion, imposed by the proportions of the instruments
in use. This is to be deplored. The size of the instrument
should never impose a *positioning* that restricts freedom of
movement. Performing on an instrument held at the shoulder
is difficult enough without adding to the miseries! I adhere
to a firm belief that there is only one way to hold the viola

in a manner that will relieve one of all tension. This position is arrived at as shown in plates 13 to 16.* Note that in plates 13 and 14 my right leg is advanced instead of left because I am, for the moment, holding the viola with the right hand. By plate 16 I am looking partly to the left. But plate 17† illustrates what I regard as an unnecessary pose. One does not really *have* to look at one's fingers, and if one persists it will amount to a pain in the neck! Likewise it is injudicious to hold the instrument in front of one as if it were a continuation of the chin as this pulls the left shoulder forward throwing it completely out of position and, again, contributing to further pains in the neck (see plate 18).‡

It is at this point that I am assailed by the fact that, as in the case of all textbooks dealing with matters which demand the subtlest of coordinated motions, where every individual student, be he violinist, violist, cellist or bassist, be he a student of golf, baseball, cricket, tennis or what you will, must be treated as an entity, the textbook must often fall short of its avowed purpose. As well indulge in the folly of a 'home cure' through the agency of a medical dictionary or *vade mecum*. However, the book has its uses if only that we all need, as Walter Pater has it, 'some imaginative stimulus, some not impossible ideal as may shape vague hope, and transform it into effective desire'. In short, the book should prompt the urge to seek the guidance of a trusted mentor. The book should, moreover, always be the adjunct to the teacher.

Size

Over the years, since it became tolerable to regard the viola as being a very definite entity, there has raged a sweeping controversy regarding the proportions of the instrument. Tertis was strongly opposed to the 'small' instrument, and at first he owned and played a 'large' Montagnana. I do not

*Plates 13–16 are opposite page 174
†Plate 17 is opposite page 175
‡Plate 18 is opposite page 175

have the dimensions to hand, but it was undoubtedly in the class over seventeen inches in length. The result of using this instrument over the years was the development of a seriously strained left arm, a sort of bursitis I assume, which drove him to retire from the public platform and to announce that he would cease to play altogether. One just could not imagine Tertis divorcing himself completely from his beloved viola in whose cause he had striven so gallantly and, to be sure, he did not. With considerable invention he planned what we all know now as the 'Tertis Model' viola, and encouraged *luthiers* all over the world to build instruments according to his particular blueprint, which was an exemplar of accuracy and came up to all his expectations. In other words, it achieved all the virtues of the 'large' viola with none of its encumbrances.

I have ever been flexible in this matter of body length. I do not hold that it is impossible for a smaller instrument to be lacking in quality or volume on the C string. That there is a difference in quality goes without argument, and it is up to the individual player, to say nothing of the individual listener, to prefer one type of sonority to another. In my own case I must confess to a strong preference for the mezzo-soprano quality over the darker contralto sound that I detect in all the 'large' instruments. For my style of playing, too, I tend to favour the brilliance experienced from my Andrea Guarneri to what I perceive to be a more recalcitrant response from the 'large' instrument. The four Guarneri violas (and, according to Hill, there are only four, all made by Andrea, he being the only member of this illustrious and innovative family to make violas) appear at first sight to be quite similar to the models by Stradivari. And indeed they are, but for one very important dimension. The middle bout is wider, and therein lies the source of the greater sonority on the lowest string as compared with Stradivari. The same difference is experienced when listening to a del Gesù violin alongside a Strad. violin. Del Gesù exploited the wide middle bout to its extremities. I stated a while back that I have always been flexible in the matter of body length, but I must confess that this flexibility is disposed to become intractable in the matter of instruments smaller than the Strad. or Guarneri dimensions. Nonetheless, if a performer can produce a fine sound (not, mark you, a loud sound) from a small instrument who am I to condemn because the instrument does not come up to certain proportions established by I know not whom? But experience has taught me not to expect a satisfactory 'viola' sound from a short model, although I find I must be on the alert, and admonish all others in this controversy, not to colour the truth with preferences.

And now I come to the problem of the ladies. It has been my recent experience, both in the United States and in Japan, that a greater number of young women are bent on studying and playing the viola than male students. Apart from evidence of innate good taste and gentle wisdom it is hard to tell why this should be so. From the outset there is the handicap encountered by reason that the average female hand is smaller and slighter than the male. The fingers are often sufficiently long but are usually quite slender with a narrow point, and as it is quite essential that the finger should be able to cover two strings at once it is necessary to alter the spacing of the strings in order to meet this requirement. If the hand is of the square, broad type it is usually too small to be used on violas of sixteen inches and over. Indeed, Tertis would deny anyone the right to play any viola as diminutive. However, as I have indicated, I am inclined to be a bit more flexible, and when I am moved by the aching desire, the urgency which drives them to play the viola – which will not be denied – I am constrained to accept them as students and trust that what the tone may lack in volume it may compensate with quality. However, I must add that the quality often lacks what we know as the 'true viola sound', and this is unfortunate. Nonetheless, when the student's mind is unshakably made up and is not to be persuaded on any other course, I cannot but feel that the best should be got out of the situation through a course of instruction which pays the closest attention to the proper use of the bow.

To sum up: I adjure violists to seek instruments not less in length than the models of Stradivari and Guarneri with an eye to those, like Guarneri's, with a wide middle bout. From that dimension up to seventeen inches I deem practical. Over seventeen inches one runs into dangerous situations. I am quite certain that it would be impossible to perform the second concerto by Darius Milhaud on the oversized viola fancied by a few players. For that matter it is almost impossible on a conventional instrument, but performing on a Brobdingnagian model provides as good an excuse as I know for not exposing oneself to its terrors. This holds true for other works which call for the higher virtuosity, the touch of the 'Notenfresser'. There are those, of course, that hold that the viola is unfitted for such displays. I don't agree! As for those situations which arise where women performers are too slight to handle instruments over sixteen inches in length, I would, in the first place, suggest that they might find it more convenient and rewarding to study the violin. But, as is usually the case, if their minds are implacably made up, then I would advise that they should seek instruments of the widest dimensions and with deep ribs. These departures from the norm sometimes make up for the shorter lineal dimension. But, avoid the oddball models that have been offered from time to time.

Repertoire

There are certain beliefs, unsupported by evidence, which have a monstrous power of survival against clear proof of their fallaciousness. One of the more durable is that which avers, again and again, that the repertoire available to us violists is exiguous, despite the evidence to the contrary offered by such a comprehensive catalogue as compiled by Professor Zeyringer in which he lists works for viola alone, viola and piano, viola and orchestra and viola in combination with all sorts of other instruments. Nevertheless the belief persists. The reason for this, I am satisfied, resides with the press. Critics who otherwise take their responsibilities seriously and strive to know what they are writing about in

respect of other solo instruments appear to have taken little
trouble to ascertain the extent of music available to the violist. How very often have I had reviews (good and otherwise)
which have qualified the praise, when the burden of the col-
umn was favourable, with something like: 'The pity is that
Mr Primrose's talent should be so circumscribed by such a
lack of material,' or words to that effect. Very often, I must
confess, players evoke such criticisms by presenting a dull,
unenterprising programme overloaded with transcriptions. I
do not disapprove of transcriptions, but whereas a violinist
can get away with a reasonable number of these in his
programme because it is well known that he is not obliged
to do this by reason of the poverty of his repertoire, a violist
would be reminded that he was *driven* to such misconduct by
the sparseness of his resources.

I beg violists to steer clear of these 'lollipops', as Lionel
Tertis is wont to call them, especially if it is a début appearance. In this connection, I am often asked what is my opinion
about the Paganini *Caprices* for the viola. Although this
comes in the category of what is known as a 'come on'
question, an attempt to lure me into, as they say in pugilistic
circles, 'leading with my chin', I find it easy to answer. If you
have the technique to play them go to it. They are loads of
fun, and make you feel superior! On the other hand, if you
do not have the ability and dexterity, then you must adopt a
very lofty attitude, a high-minded posture and imply that
never, never would you stoop to such meretricious folly, so
distinguished is your musical discretion.

To return to the more sober moment: I do not feel it
necessary to offer a list of works suitable for public presentation based on my own experience. There are a number of
catalogues which list the important works available, the most
important being the compilation mentioned above by Professor Zeyringer, founder of the *Viola-Forschungsgesellschaft*.
But even this mine of information is not comprehensive or
up-to-date. The numerous additions to the viola repertoire
by British composers are known to all my British readers, and
it has been my purpose, since I have lived the greater part of

my life abroad, to bring them to the attention of players and public in other lands. And, of course, we all know of the great contribution of Paul Hindemith. But there are other German composers who merit attention, and I would strongly recommend the remarkable concerto for viola, piano and orchestra by the late Karl Amadeus Hartmann of Munich.

The late Quincy Porter, Professor of Composition at Yale University, and a very accomplished violist himself, some years ago wrote for me what I consider to be one of the most engaging of all viola concertos. His piece for unaccompanied viola also merits attention.

The work of Japanese composers is not widely known beyond these Islands (I am writing this from Tokyo), but they are surprisingly versatile and contemporary in thought and style. Surprising, that is, to one who has not lived in Japan and become aware, as I have, of the boundless activity and interest in everything to do with music, and the almost stratospheric level of instrumental talent. I mention at random the concerto by Sadao Bekku, a student of Milhaud, Messiaen and Jean Rivier, and a sonata for viola and piano by Kan Ishii, a graduate of the Staatliche Akademie für Tonkunst in Munich.

Our repertoire is almost entirely lacking in works of the Romantic period. However, the very early sonata by Mendelssohn has some utterly charming moments. The one by Glinka is occasionally rewarding, and the works of Max Bruch and Joachim are worthy of inclusion in a recital programme. I must also mention the vast field of baroque music to be explored. To be sure not a little of it is for instruments that are similar to the viola, such as the viola d'amore and others, but it is music which is singularly conformable to the viola and, of course, there are many works for the viola itself. The patient researcher will glean a rewarding harvest. No, I do not agree that we need sit hungry at our own table when the feast of music is under way.

Now there are two other aspects to be remembered in all this cataloguing of our resources. They are chamber music and the orchestra. And what a vast table of riches we have here. I must confess it was the bewitchery of chamber music which seduced me to the viola many years ago – a seduction I have never regretted. That I spent many years on the solo platform was, in a sense, by chance. Not an urgency; not a craving for public acclaim. Realizing my woeful inexperience in the orchestra, and understanding the important role the viola plays in this aggregation, I made it my business, without any hesitation, to accept an invitation to join the prestigious ranks of the violists recruited to serve Toscanini in the legendary NBC orchestra in 1937, a group that I stayed with for four engrossing and rewarding years. So, the young violist may rest assured that so far as available music is concerned he need not worry lest he exhaust his store before he exhaust himself.

Teaching and vibrato

Now that I approach the end of my little treatise on the viola, and things to do with string playing, I am assailed by the fact that so many factors have not been touched upon, but which could scarcely have been treated in such a little voyage of enquiry which has, even now, almost reached its 'butt and sea mark'. Such things as problems of psychology involved in teaching, with its concomitant problem of teaching a student how to practise. This latter problem is, in my judgement, one of the most important of a teacher's duties. The importance of *thinking* first, and then, playing. The matter of stance, with the back straight, the shoulders open and on an equal and level plane, the feet placed as wide as the shoulders of the player, the left foot a little in advance with the weight poised towards the front of the foot, and never resting ponderously on the heels. Then there is the completely different body set-up when playing sitting down – again a matter of balance, with a strict admonition against allowing the spine to touch and recline on the back of the chair, and curing this fault by having the student practise sitting on a piano stool; and a further admonition never to tuck the feet (crossed or otherwise) under the seat, but in front with the left foot advanced even more than when standing.

There is a host of other things. Vibrato, for example. I think I have this question put to me more often than any other by anxious and perplexed students: how should it be practised? how should it be developed? what speed should it attain? and so forth. And to observe their disappointment when I tell them that vibrato will never be of any use to them until they are able to execute an impeccable bow-stroke. That vibrato has two functions: first, to express the aesthetic urges and impulses of the player, in which case it will almost always be a *natural* one which springs unbidden and does not require practice; and second, a device to enhance the beauty of the tone, which, in turn, is just not there to be enhanced if the player does not know how to draw the bow successfully. I know of no way to teach a completely satisfactory vibrato. Certainly, vibrato can be taught, but I can always differentiate between the one that is taught, no matter how ingeniously, and the natural vibrato which I am convinced all our front rank virtuosi possess. And how fascinating it is to reflect that, like thumb prints, no two are alike. Hence the eternal enchantment afforded the listener in apprehending the spirit of each differing player. I may be specific, however, in saying that in playing viola one should use an arm vibrato almost exclusively. A wrist vibrato produces too rapid an oscillation to be satisfactorily perceived by the ear of the listener. Its speed, too, should vary according to the dictates of the inspiration excited by the piece being played, and, of course, the aesthetic nature of each player. Apart from these opinions and counsel I have nothing to add.

Coda

In closing I must confess that the task Mr Menuhin so graciously asked me to undertake has been no task at all. It has been immensely rewarding, and has afforded me a deep pleasure, not the least of the satisfaction derived from being associated with him between the covers of this book. There are those, I have no doubt, who will suggest that I appear, at times, dogmatic and opinionated. So be it. A man without opinions and the courage to give them utterance is a faint and feeble creature, and to fear to appear dogmatic in their utterance is to fail in what I am persuaded is a bounden duty. Some, who like to ingest their learning in ponderous fashion, may hint that I am guilty of unseemly levity. But then, I have in my time suffered from what I call the 'Herr Professor' approach to didactics, and shy away from inflicting it on others.

I hold with the late Max Beerbohm (the incomparable Max) that it is 'strange, when you come to think of it, that of all the countless folk who have lived before our time on this planet not one is known in history or legend as having died of laughter'. There were moments, I must concede, when I hesitated to introduce some pleasantry, calling to mind, as I did, Max saying, on another occasion, something to the effect that one should not show one's humour to the humourless lest they use it against you. (I do not remember his exact words.) But, now and then I have been comforted in the knowledge that anyone who plays on a string instrument at the shoulder must have a superb sense of the ridiculous and be, himself, an exuberant repository of humour.

Part Three

A Short History*
by Denis Stevens

*A comprehensive history of the violin would
not only fill a complete tome; it would also be
outside the scope of this series. It has therefore
been decided to concentrate on some perhaps
less well-known aspects.

Twelve
Early History

Introduction

Given the bare minimum of incipient biographical information, or the slender evidence of an autograph score, a musical
scholar worthy of his calling would not find it too difficult to
tell a composer's date and place of birth from a legible *acte
de naissance*, nor would he find it too hazardous to venture a
reasonable guess at a period of composition after studying
handwriting, style and watermarks enshrined in the leaves at
his disposal. Ask that same scholar to supply the name of the
town and the approximate year in which any instrument of the
Middle Ages or the Renaissance was invented, and he will at
once admit defeat.

Instruments, like humans, evolved slowly, and, although
the rate of their evolution hardly bears comparison, the
principles involved are not dissimilar. Changes seem to take
place in silence and mystery; and the new so often bears the
firm stamp of inevitability that an actual change is not
noticed until long after the event. The more commonly used
and widely practised the instrument is, the harder it becomes
to pin down its true origin. In the case of the violin, we find
– as indeed we might expect – the violin itself, a bow and
some resin. The ancillary materials are important because it
has often been suggested that this most perfect of stringed and
bowed instruments could be traced back to the Greek kithara.

The shape, construction and technique of the kithara differ
so much from the various attributes of the violin that any
attempt to relate the two instruments must be classed with the
kind of pseudo-philology which derives the word virgin from

vir (Latin) and *gin* (Old English) with the resulting connotation of man-trap. Notwithstanding the occasional use of plucked-string effects on the violin and other members of its family, the distinguishing feature and crowning beauty of its tonal capabilities has always resided – and will doubtless so continue to reside – in its unmatched cantilena, made possible only by the skilful wielding of a bow.

Bowed string instruments have enjoyed a wide geographical distribution for many thousands of years. The reason for their universal use and popularity is not difficult to understand, since the principle of a continually resonant string amplified by a hollow body is both simple and basic in almost all cultures. A discussion and comparison of the countless varieties known to us through past illustrations or present customs would demand the kind of open-ended scholarly investigation normally reserved for vast projects in science or literature. It is, however, possible to show some of the main interactions and influences in a very general sense, limiting the area of enquiry to Asia and Central Europe.

One probable and plausible cradle for the simplest kind of violin is Kurdestan, for the medieval Persian fiddles are said to have come from there, and the Chinese variety (related to the bowed zither or lute) was apparently introduced by the barbarian tribes from the West. In India the more sophisticated sarangi, with its sympathetic strings, held sway in the northern part of the country, while in the south the sarinda maintained its popularity because of its relative technical simplicity. The spike-fiddle, so easy to carry over the shoulder, won most supporters in Islam, while in Finland and Estonia it was the bowed lyre that attracted most attention. In Byzantium the bowed lyre boasted a drone, and the player made considerable use of natural harmonics. Each national fiddle had its own peculiar form and its own special manner of playing.

Exactly how and when the fiddle was brought to Western Europe must remain open questions. In spite of the wealth of evidence in support of an Asian origin, consideration should also be given to the part played by Arabian instruments that were taken over by medieval musicians in Spain and brought eventually to Italy. Nor can one ignore the role played by the Polish fiddles, by the Bulgarian gadulka, by the Russian gudok and smyk, portrayed in frescoes as early as the eleventh century. Such instruments were often played in a manner not too far removed from the modern violinist's chin and shoulder grip, for their leading exponents were shepherds who liked to coax melodies from their fiddles as they walked through the countryside.

To add to the confusion of historians, the polymorphous nature of the violin seems to have inspired a complementary terminological farrago embracing hundreds of different languages and dialects. Words have been bent, twisted, adapted, transformed, and modified in all the accepted ways and quite a few unorthodox ones, so that the study of comparative literature as it refers to bowed string instruments throughout the ages not infrequently poses more questions than it answers.

Terminology

By sampling some of the words used for bowed string instruments in medieval England, the extent of the terminological and philological problems can be easily appreciated. When the word viol makes its appearance in the late fifteenth century, the reference is definitely to a soft-toned, flat-back instrument played in the sitting position. There is no hint of the word violin until the reign of Henry VIII. But something very much like the violin existed, and its name was fydyl (with such variant spellings as fydell, fithele, fedyll, fethill, vythule), the derivation from medieval Latin vidula being both clear and obvious. This instrument was played with a fydylstyk, a sure proof that it was bowed and not plucked. It probably had only three strings, tuned in fifths, and its finger-board lacked the frets that are essential to the viol and lute families. Most important was the use to which it was generally put, and in this it resembled the later violin – dancing, banquets, betrothals and other social events called for a strong and penetrating sound, preferably produced from an instrument held shoulder-high as an aid to projection.

The earliest recorded appearance of the word seems to be in the earlier of two manuscripts of a legendary history of Britain written in the early thirteenth century by a Worcestershire priest. Layamon's *Brut* contains the following line: 'Ne cuðe na mon swa muchel of song of harpe & of salterium: of fiðele & of coriu.' Towards the end of that same century, a Legendary from the south-eastern part of England includes these words in a life of St Thomas the Apostle: 'At þis bruydale was plei i-nouȝh: song and gret hoppingue, Tabours and fiþele and symphanye.' Written down about the year 1300, the Auchinleck manuscript of *Sir Beues of Hamtoun* mentions the kind of music played on these early fiddles: 'While Iosian was in Ermonie, ȝhe hadde lerned of minstralcie, Vpon a fiþele for to play Staumpes, notes, garibles gay.' In our own terminology, dances, songs, and lively variations.

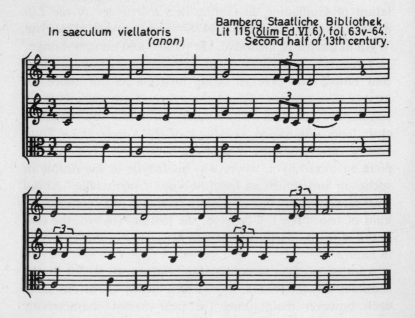

In saeculum viellatoris
(anon)

Bamberg Staatliche Bibliothek, Lit 115 (olim Ed. VI.6), fol. 63v–64. Second half of 13th century.

By the middle of the fifteenth century muddled morphology begins to rear its familiar head, for vocabularies compiled at this time appear to equate the fiddle with the rybybe, which had an oval body and four strings. The variants vitula and uetella are both associated with the rybybe, while vidula is said to be a vythule. Worse still, a fedylle is aligned with the medieval Latin term viella, whose French equivalent could mean either a bowed string instrument or its mechanical counterpart, the hurdy-gurdy. A three-part composition of the early thirteenth century (see page 196), written in France, has the title 'In seculum viellatoris', which may simply mean the version of 'In seculum' (part of the Easter gradual *Haec dies*) used by a player of the vielle.

Nevertheless, the fiddle made itself heard above the din of dinner and even above the blare of brass and percussion. Contemporaneous with those vocabularies, the story of *King Ponthus and the Fair Sidonie* tells us that 'the mete was ordaned and ther was dyuers mynstrelleses, of trumpes, taboretes, and fydelles'. This humble role seems to have been shared by the rybyble, if we can trust John Lydgate's translation of Guillaume de Guilleville's *Pilgrimage of the Life of Man*, usually dated about 1425: 'And to revelle at taverne, Wyth al merthe & mellodye, On rebube and on symphonye.' In Lydgate's earlier *Reson and Sensuallyte* the implication is that bowed and plucked string instruments are 'more for estatys than taverns.' Could the rybybe have sunk so far in less than two decades? The similarity of fiddle and rybyble is clear from this line in *The Book of the Knight of La Tour-Landry*, also from the mid-fifteenth century: 'The said Sir piere . . . axed hym, where was his fedylle or his ribible or suche an instrument as longithe vnto a mynstralle.' About 1500 *Herkyn to my tale* contains a reference to a very unusual kind of trio: 'The fox fydylyd, the ratton rybybyd, the lark notyd with all.' Virtuoso man had begun to experience rivalry in nature.

Another popular bowed string instrument played at the shoulder was the rebeck, known as a family of various sizes, each however maintaining the pear-shaped characteristic

197

and the customary three strings. One of Lydgate's shorter poems, *A Mumming at Hertford*, suggests that the player could simultaneously sing: 'He with his rebecke may sing ful offt ellas!' The German word for fiddle was *Geige*, which was taken over in Old French as *gigue*, the player being described as a *gigueor*; and this in turn passed into the English language as gigeur. The earliest of three manuscripts of *King Horn* (about 1250-60) has the phrase 'Hi weren harpurs, & sume were gigours', but the word never gained currency since most people preferred fiddle in one or other of its numerous spellings.

Quite obviously, the Geige, rybybe, rebeck, and fiddle were closely interrelated, and the quest for improvement and perfection led makers to combine the best and most practical features of all of them into an instrument that allowed easy access of the bow to all strings, a full and healthy tone and guaranteed ease of portability. In the sixteenth century violinists were often confused with rebeck players, and the rebeck was sometimes called lira. In 1581 Vincenzo Galilei (father of the astronomer and mathematician) spoke of the 'viola da braccio, which not so many years ago was called lira da braccio' in his *Dialogo* concerning the differences between old and new music. Words changed, the number of strings grew or diminished according to fashion, but the controlling feature, in more senses than one, was the bow.

Repertoire: manuscript music

Anybody who has studied musical manuscripts written before the mid-sixteenth century knows that even those parts or lines obviously intended for instrumental performance never name the instrument. Orchestration in those days was an unpredictable, aleatory affair; and in consequence the actual sound of any given composition would vary quite considerably from one performance to another. Even in our era of standardized scores, the timbre of an orchestra in Vienna is subtly but recognizably different from that of its counterpart in Paris, and that in turn offers a tonal palette at variance with an orchestra in London or New York. How much greater therefore must the differences have been in the Middle Ages and in the Renaissance! The director of music at a court or chapel, the leader of the band at a dance, the chief minstrel in a masque or other entertainment – all these had to decide how the music at their disposal should be performed, and quite naturally they were limited by the number and quality of their personnel or, in some cases, given a free hand by some munificent Maecenas and thus able to indulge their wildest fantasies, as in the Florentine intermezzi of 1589.

The so-called mystery of violin repertoire in early times, or rather the mystery of what the predecessors of the violin actually played, is a recurring one in that any given century yields a vast quantity of music in which instruments obviously took part, either on their own or with voices; and at the same time documents, diaries, letters, paintings and illuminations prove beyond a shadow of doubt that bowed string families of instruments were constantly in use, though the music they had to play is never mentioned by title. On the one hand, music without instrumental designation; on the other, instruments without repertoire.

The principles to be followed in solving this problem are at the same time simple and scientific. We know that the rebeck and its variants were popular in dance ensembles, and we know that France had its estampies and danses royales, Italy its saltarelli and trotti, England its duple- and triple-time dances even though the titles are rarely given. All that remains to be done is to check the total range of notes in each part, and match this with the range of the instruments. If these agree – and in the majority of cases they do – it is reasonable to assume that the music could have been played by such-and-such an ensemble.

There were of course such hybrids as broken consorts, to borrow a term from later Elizabethan England, these being a mixture of wind and stringed instruments, bowed and plucked. Not infrequently the ranges of a wind and a stringed instrument will coincide, and it may be argued that because of

199

this no particular instrumentation is provable. This is perfectly true. But the object of the exercise is not so much to prove that the rebeck or the fiddle must have played a certain line of music, but that it could have done so if the player had been asked by his director. To prove the matter otherwise would be to remove from our present-day performers the opportunity of enjoying that same freedom and privilege enjoyed by the minstrels of earlier times.

In fact all medieval dance tunes sound well on stringed instruments. The penetrating, nasal tone of the rebeck is perfect for music requiring incisive rhythm and regular accent. There are, however, many other uses for this versatile family of near-violins. It can suitably sustain a part in polyphonic song, which flourished from the time of Adam de la Hale (*c*. 1250–*c*. 1306) until the consort song declined in the second half of the sixteenth century – three hundred years of music embracing the finest creations of Machaut, Landini, Dufay, Dunstable, Ockeghem, Josquin, Tromboncino, Cornyshe and Stolzer, to name only nine out of ninety or more composers who wrote in the current idiom of accompanied song. To pretend that fiddles were not used in this repertoire would be tantamount to claiming that the lute was an unessential element in seventeenth-century song, or the piano in the Romantic era.

The unessential element was in fact the voice. If there were no singer, the instrument nearest in range (whether treble in the case of the Italian *frottola* or tenor in the case of the German *Tenorlied*) would act as substitute. Songs by no means negligible in number have come down to us in manuscripts such as the Glogau Liederbuch or in printed editions such as *Harmonice Musices Odhecaton A*, but they are either completely deprived of text or possess no means of identification beyond a tantalisingly laconic incipit. It is very likely that they were considered as material for instrumental performance, and even more likely that their uppermost part would have been played by a fiddle (see p. 201). A similar and comparable case is presented by religious music, especially motets and isolated sections of the *ordinarium missae*.

Dit le bourguignon *(anon)*

Petrucci: Harmonice Musices
Odhecaton A (1501), fol. 20v

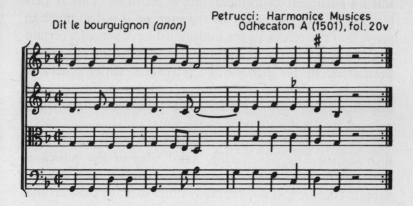

Benvenuto Cellini, who was a musician in his youth, speaks of playing motets in a wind-band; and the extraction and popularization of the *In nomine Domini* section from John Taverner's Mass *Gloria tibi Trinitas* started a fashion in chamber-music circles that did not decline until the time of Purcell.

Musical repertoire was to a considerable extent interchangeable and adaptable. But there always remained a small nucleus of works whose stylistic features or descriptive title clearly indicated performance by instruments exclusively. There is, for example, a single purely instrumental piece in the enormously impressive collection of songs in the Cancionero de Palacio (Royal Library, Madrid) – a dance entitled *Alta* by Francisco de la Torre. There are just two instrumental works (untitled) among the thousands of items contained in the seven great choirbooks at Trento: both in volume 89, and both written on the eight-line staves that were traditionally reserved for instruments with wide ranges. There are English pieces such as *Quene Note*, copied on the back of an astronomical table of the early fifteenth century, and German dances with fanciful names, such as *Der kranich schnabel*, *Der natter schwanz*, *Der neue bauern schwanz* – these three in the songbook from Glogau in Upper Silesia. Most of these sound extremely well when played by a consort of bowed strings, ancient or modern (see p. 202).

Der pfauen schwanz
(anon)

Berlin: Oeffentliche wissens-
chaftliche Bibliothek, Z.98 No. 208

Repertoire: printed music

The first glimmer of light from the dawn of the sixteenth century discovered the birth of the art of printing polyphonic music. Significantly enough, Petrucci's first anthology – the *Odhecaton* of 1501 – contained numerous three- and four-part compositions ripe and ready for instrumental performance, and others were not slow to follow his lead. It was a critical time for the violin, too, for the Venetian *luthier* Giovanni Maria della Corna (originally from Brescia) had begun to specialize in the lira da braccio, uncannily close to the violin in shape though larger in size and provided with five strings and two drones. On such an instrument polyphony was not only possible but desirable, and we learn from descriptions of skilled performers – Alessandro Striggio, for instance – that the kind of part-writing best known from Bach's sonatas for unaccompanied violin must already have been in existence in the mid-sixteenth century. Striggio was said to have played on the 'viola' (almost certainly a lira da braccio) four parts simultaneously with such elegance and fullness of tone that listeners were amazed.

Nobody, unfortunately, knows what music he played. But there is abundant printed music in three and four parts, some of it in separate partbooks and some in tablature, so that any capable executant could transcribe whatever he needed.

Striggio the elder, however, was more than a capable executant: he was a composer whose works were held in high esteem,
and he would have enjoyed the challenge of writing music for
his favourite stringed instrument. The lira da braccio might
be described as the perfect tonal vehicle for bowed polyphony, just as the lute was for the plucked-string family of
instruments. The ricercare and fantasia were the forms that
suited it best, for they called for rich sonority and evenness of
tone-production.

In the early 1520s the violin began to make its appearance
in documents and in paintings. Players of the *violon* from
Vercelli are mentioned in the account-books of the court of
Emmanuele Filiberto, Duke of Savoy; and in that same
Piedmontese town the church of San Cristoforo contains a
painting by Gaudenzio Ferrari, 'La Madonna degli aranci',
in which a child is playing a small violin – not a rebeck, nor
yet a lira da braccio, but an instrument not too different in
shape from the later classic models. This beautiful painting is
usually dated 1529-30, and it is surely no coincidence that at
precisely this time the Parisian music publisher Pierre Attaign-
ant was following up his earlier successes in lute books by
issuing the first printed anthologies of dance music: *Six
Gaillardes et six Pavanes*, and *Neuf basses dances deux
branles vingt et cinq Pavennes avec quinze Gaillardes*, each
publication consisting of four partbooks in mensural notation, which would have been given out to the individual
performers in just the same way that the parts of a string
quartet are handed round before a rehearsal today.

No instruments are mentioned anywhere in Attaingnant's
anthologies, but the fact that the violin was so highly prized
as a member of dance-music ensembles, combined with the
evidence of a 'violin range' in the uppermost part, suggests
that this is very probably the sort of music a violinist would
have to deal with if he were looking for repertoire in the early
1530s. In Germany Hans Gerle's *Musica Teusch* (1532)
devoted its third section to the violin family, then known as
kleine Geigen in contradistinction to *grosse Geigen* which
meant fretted viols. The matter is neatly summed up by the

author's own words: '*Hie hebt an der Drittayl diss Buchs und lernt wie du solt auff den kleynen Geigleyn lernen die kein Bündt haben*'; ('here begins the third part of this book, and it teaches you how you should study the violins that have no frets'). Two four-part pieces are given in this edition, and two different ones in the revised and augmented edition of 1546.

Gerle's original lead was followed up in 1538 by the Nuremberg publisher, Hieronymus Formschneider, whose *Trium vocum carmina* could be considered as a kind of German *Odhecaton*, since there are exactly one hundred compositions. Not one of them has text, title or composer's name appended, but the tenor partbooks of the two surviving copies (Jena and Berlin) provide scattered marginalia showing that late-fifteenth as well as early-sixteenth-century composers are well represented. A lengthy Latin preface explains that text has been omitted because pure sound increases the pleasure of the listener; and this may be one of the first references to the possibilities of aural rapture inherent in all good instrumental music. Most of the items in this collection can be played by a string trio of one kind or another, and much of the music in the discant partbook lies well in the violin range.

In view of the close association between the development of violin-making and the north Italian towns of Brescia and Cremona, it is worth pausing for a closer look at two pioneering publications by a Cremonese composer, Agostino Licino. In 1545 and 1546 he produced two volumes of 'chromatic duos' (a reference to black notes, not purple harmony) containing forty-five compositions in all, each one being in strict canon. One might guess that this apparently monotonous contrapuntal diet smelt of the lamp of some obdurate theorist, but a glance at the second volume – the only one provided with a dedication – clearly demonstrates that such a guess would be wildly wrong. Licino really expected his duos to be performed for pleasure, and expressed the hope that his patron Benedetto Guarna of Salerno would play them over with his family and friends instead of indulging in *primero*, a popular card game immortalized in music by Alessandro Striggio. He goes on to say that he hopes the canons 'will be of no little help in learning to play bowed string instruments, such as viols and violins and other similar instruments'.

The words he uses are '*uiole uioloni* & *altri stromenti simili*', which raises once more the familiar question about the derivation of the word violin, and the apparent relationship between *violone* (the usual Italian term for double-bass) and *violon*, which is the classic French word for the violin. The probable explanation is that the Italians took the opposite point of view from the Germans, for whom *Kleingeige* signified the violin family, while *Grossgeige* stood for the chest of viols. What was small to the Germans was large to the Italians: the usual suffix for bigness ('*-one*') yielded *violone*, which was then applied indiscriminately to all sizes of violin, while viola referred exclusively to the viols. Diagrammatically this early stage in the philology of the violin would appear thus:

German	Italian	French
Kleingeige	*violone*	*violon*
Grossgeige	*viola*	*viole*

Perhaps the Italian suffix denoted at first not so much physical size as bigness of sound, the meaning undergoing a subtle change when people realized the anomaly of calling a small instrument a *violone*. Unconsciously following the Germans, they began to acknowledge the violin as a small member of a large family, and substituted the diminutive suffix resulting in the word *violino*. By this time it was too late to change the French vowels, so that *violon* survives to the present day; but the more conservative English waited for the newer Italian term and coined violin from *violino*, a reasonably accurate and not too difficult accomplishment. Although the professional philologists, with their theories about phonemes and metathesis and assimilation, may continue to debate over these peculiarities for many decades, it is unlikely that a totally convincing explanation will ever be found for all the

205

possible variants and corruptions of those basic terms. Some
secrets, after all, must remain inviolate.

Attaingnant, encouraged by the welcome accorded to his
earlier publications, issued a book of fifty dances in 1547,
this time with all the separate parts printed in the old choir-
book fashion, so that four players (only one item calls for
five) could play from the open book (see below).

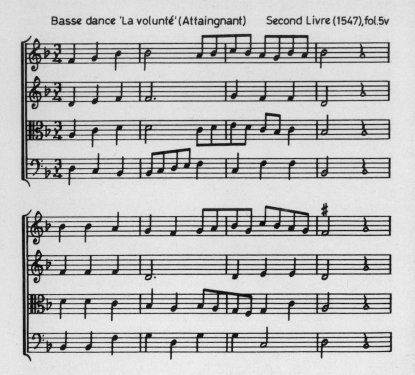

Basse dance 'La volunté' (Attaingnant)   Second Livre (1547), fol. 5v

No specific instruments are mentioned in this collection, nor
in the volume of trios by Willaert and Tiburtino, published at
Venice in 1549, which is stated to be 'for singing and playing
with every kind of instrument'. The hexachord fantasias by
Tiburtino and the ricercari by Willaert are more suited for
viols than for violins, though it is not impossible that they
were occasionally performed by a mixed consort. The
Venetian composer Jacques Buus, originally from Flanders,
composed a number of four-part ricercari about this time,

Plate 19. Medieval viol player

19

casting his performance net even wider than that of his contemporaries: the music is 'for singing, playing on the organ and other instruments'.

Such calculated vagueness of intention may tantalize the scholar in search of pure violin music, but his persistence is to some extent rewarded by a definite mention of violins on the title-page of an undated work, *Musique de Joye*, published at Lyon by Jacques Moderne. Circumstances point to a date not earlier than 1547, and not later than 1556. Once again the performance media suggest an almost commercial breadth of outlook, for the dances and ricercari are '*appropriée tant à la voix humaine, que pour apprendre à sonner Espinetes, Violons, & Fleustes*'. Leaving aside for the moment the various vocal possibilities, it would certainly be possible to take the publisher at his word and organize a mixed consort of recorders and violins, with a spinet providing a rudimentary 'basso seguente'. Moderne borrowed several of his ricercari from an earlier Venetian publication, *Musica nova* ('for organs and other instruments'), besides taking a few dances from Attaingnant, but this ranked as normal behaviour in an era not exactly famous for its observance of copyright.

By mid-century the violin was well established, and hitherto hesitant publishers opened the flood-gates of their ubiquitous presses so that no musician could possibly complain about a lack of repertoire, especially for dancing. The indefatigable Attaingnant issued five further volumes of dances, no longer by anonymous composers, between 1550 and 1557, the principal contributors being Claude Gervaise and Etienne du Tertre. In spite of the number of copies printed, these books are now of excessive rarity, and only one copy survives of each edition. Still there is no mention of violins, but their increasing participation in dance ensembles is indicated by paintings and engravings of the time, as well as in diaries and documents. A careful examination of the ranges of all the uppermost parts in dances by Gervaise reveals the fact that he rarely writes below middle C, which may explain the popularity of three-stringed violins tuned c' g' d", and it must not be forgotten in this connection that certain of the

Plate 20. Medieval pear-shaped fiddle   207

earliest Amati violins are assumed to have had only three strings originally, although they have of course been subsequently modified for modern use.

A special kind of violin used by dancing-masters was the pochette, so called because of the ease with which it could be carried in the long pocket of a dress coat. This instrument too was generally tuned in fifths though it had but three strings, and it should be noted that it ranks as an octave-transposing instrument like the piccolo, the sounds being one octave higher than written. Iconographical sources of various kinds show that it was occasionally used in ensembles as well as in formal dance-instruction, so that players of the pochette might also have found Attaingnant's collections interesting and valuable. Most surviving specimens of the pochette are of the long and narrow variety, and are usually referred to as boat-shaped, but a few genuine small violins by some of the greatest makers, including Guarnerius del Gesù, point to a wider use of the individual members of the violin family than is generally supposed, as well as a broader interpretation of the term pochette.

Several collections of instrumental pieces, many of them doubtless intended for the use of budding violinists, sport fanciful, amusing, or bizarre titles among their contents. Francesco Bendusi's *Opera Nova de Balli* (1553) offers such gems as 'La Mala vecchia', 'Bella foresta', and (significantly, perhaps) 'Violla', though the title-page bears the usual catch-all phrase tempting all instrumentalists, no matter what their special interest might be. In 1560 the Sicilian composer Pietro Vinci issued a volume of duos featuring such names as 'Coccocino', 'Gallina ratto rattonis', and 'La Vaccarra'; while four years later Vincenzo Ruffo compiled a book of trios – *Capricci in Musica* – full of such things as 'La brava', 'El perfidioso', and 'El Trapolato'. At a later stage it was customary to entitle works in honour of a friend or patron, as the Cremonese composer Tarquinio Merula did in his *Primo Libro delle Canzoni a Quattro Voci per sonare con ogni sorte de strumenti musicali* (1615), the first item 'La Ghirardella' referring to the dedicatee, Giovanni Pietro Ghirardello, and another 'La Monteverde' to a famous son of Merula's home town.

The extent and variety of this repertoire cannot be over-stressed, nor can its importance for the violin be under-estimated. If a popular instrument exists at a time when no music appears to have been written expressly for it, and if at the same point in history a vast flood of music bursts upon the scene without any particular instrumental designation, it is only logical to assume that at least some of the music (in this case dance-music) was played by the violins, and that in consequence our modern performances of these works should include violinists – not viol-players, whose preferred and proper pursuit is the fantasia and its allied forms.

Tielman Susato in Antwerp followed the French example by publishing a volume of dances, all for an unspecified four-part ensemble but '*bequaem om spelen op alle musicale Instrumenten*' in 1551, and the fashion was taken up with typical Teutonic thoroughness by the brothers Paul and Bartholomew Hessen (Breslau 1555), whose two massive anthologies contain 477 compositions for ensembles ranging from four to six instruments ('*auff alle Instrument dienstlich*') and ranging internationally over Spanish, Italian, English, French, German and Polish repertoire. In France Jean d'Estrées issued four books of miscellaneous dances scored for '*tous instruments musicalz*' in groups of four to six, be-tween the years 1559 and 1564. Although he was oboe player to the King of France, he would have expected violins as well as wind instruments to play the top line of his bransles, pavans, galliards and allemandes. Many of his dances, along with those of Susato, were taken over in the anthologies of Pierre Phalèse, beginning with Book I in 1571. The idea of singing as well as playing these dances still appears occa-sionally on title-pages, and even in dedications or prefaces such as that of Don Giorgio Mainerio, whose *Primo Libro de Balli* (1578) was intended for singing and for playing on all kinds of instruments. There is no doubt, however, that most of the pieces would sound really convincing only when per-formed by instruments capable of crisp attack and a lively projection of rhythms. The first item in the book, 'La Billiarda', honours its dedicatee, Monsignor Oratio Billiardo, a canon of the cathedral and a member of the Accademia de Filarmonici at Parma. Other pieces bear titles pointing to the country of origin for a particular dance ('Tedesca', 'Ungaresca' [see below], 'Ballo Francese'), or to some song or

Ungaresca (Giorgio Mainerio)   Il Primo Libro de Balli (1578), p. 16

character once popular and widely known ('Caro ortolano', 'Schiarazula Marazula').

Vincenzo Galilei, who has already been mentioned in connection with the viola da braccio, published a set of contrapuntal duets in 1584 with the aid of his son Michelangnolo, whose brief preface stresses the role of the 'viola' just as the picture of a lute and viola da braccio on the title-page throws light on the growing acceptance of bowed string instruments. These and other 'perfect instruments' could often be found in the houses of wealthy citizens or government officials, and were put to good use in musical evenings which resounded to the music of broken consorts played by the '*sonatori eccellentissimi*' mentioned in Giacomo Vincenzi's dedication of a collection of *canzoni francese* to the councillor Pietro Antonio Diedo in 1588. Arbeau's *Orchésographie* (1589) hints that violinists were expensive in the previous generation, when musicians doubling on pipe and tabor could make quite enough noise for a dance hall of moderate size. Almost certainly a clear distinction was made between formal and informal occasions, the latter having to make do with simple, rough-and-ready music. At weddings and similar occasions more money was available to hire the professional violinists who were able to demand high fees.

The twelve partbooks of Giovanni Gabrieli's *Sacrae*

Symphoniae of 1597 are of unusual interest in that definite guidance is given to performers in the matter of instrumentation, which had hitherto been left largely to chance. Both the *Canzon per sonar Quarti Toni* and the renowned *Sonata pian & forte* contain a part for '*violino*', but the range of this instrument dips below the usual g, indicating that a viola da braccio would have been more appropriate since it possessed a bottom string akin to that of a modern viola. Quite clearly terminology was still in a state of flux. Sponga (a pupil of Gabrieli), Banchieri, Vecchi, Bariolla and Mazzi all wrote instrumental music during the last decade of the century, but none of them specified the instruments that should take part. In Florence, however, the music of Malvezzi and others called for various kinds of carefully specified bowed string instruments in the intermezzi for Girolamo Bargagli's play *La Pellegrina*. This splendid musical and dramatic feast was given in honour of the wedding of Fernando Medici and Christine of Lorraine in 1589, publication following two years later.

Several excellent virtuosi took part in this production, and thanks to contemporaneous accounts of two observers the names of three violinists are known: Giovanni Battista Iacomelli, Alessandro Striggio, and his son (at that time sixteen years old) also called Alessandro, though usually given the more familiar diminutive 'Sandrino'. The presence of both father and son has not hitherto been noticed, since the father has sometimes been excluded on the grounds that he died before 1589 (the correct date of 1592 has been discovered by Professor Pierre Tagmann), and the son because he was too young. The documents, however, make it clear that both took part, for 'Io che l'onde raffreno' was accompanied by a consort including an arciviolata lira 'touched by the masterly hand of the famous Alessandro Striggio'. Such a phrase would not have been used of a youngster. Another piece, a six-part sinfonia, featured '*una violina*' played by 'Alessandrino', a diminutive that could hardly be applied to an elderly composer. Although the violin is referred to frequently, a sinfonia in the first of the six intermezzi

211

(see below) includes among its instruments a '*sopranino*

Sinfonia, Intermedio II (Luca Marenzio) Intermedii et Concerti (1591), Superius p.13

da viola', which is exactly the reverse of Gabrieli's terminology. He uses the word *violino* to mean a viola, whereas the Florentine writer uses *viola* to mean violin.

In London Antony Holborne composed a set of pavans, galliards, almains and airs 'for Viols, Violins, or other Musicall Winde Instruments', which were published in five partbooks in 1599. This deliberately imprecise instrumentation is in marked contrast to that of Thomas Morley's First Book of Consort Lessons, issued in the same year. Morley specifies a broken consort consisting of treble viol, viola da gamba, flute, cittern, lute and bandora, thus balancing precisely his three sustaining instruments with three plucked instruments (see below). An ensemble virtually identical

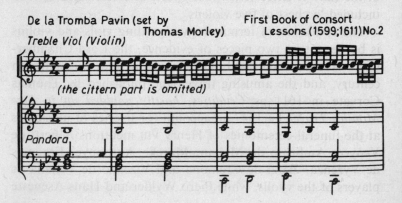

De la Tromba Pavin (set by Thomas Morley) First Book of Consort Lessons (1599;1611) No.2

Treble Viol (Violin)

(the cittern part is omitted)

Pandora

to this one may be seen in the section of the Unton Mural (in the National Portrait Gallery, London) which depicts a masque, with costumed actors surrounding a circle of six musicians all of whose instruments are visible except one. Points of interest are the use of a cross-flute (not a recorder) and of a violin (not a viol) – the latter is held against the player's chest, after the prevailing fashion of folk-fiddlers in eastern Europe and western America. The mural is named after Sir Henry Unton (*c.* 1557-96), who served as ambassador to France and would therefore have enjoyed numerous opportunities to witness the elaborate court entertainments, all of which gave music a place of special importance.

A similar ensemble had provided some of the music heard by Queen Elizabeth when she stayed as the guest of Edward Seymour, Earl of Hertford, at his manor of Elvetham in Hampshire in 1591. And once again the treble violin is mentioned, perhaps because the word 'violin' was still too new and unassimilated into the general vocabulary. Documentary references are certainly few and far between, and some of the spellings used are more than odd. In 1561, for instance, the prelude to Act I of Sackville and Norton's tragedy *Gorboduc* was played by 'violenze', which almost suggests that the string-players of those days were renowned for their attack. Thomas Kytson, a wealthy landowner and music-lover, possessed among his collection of instruments 'one boarded chest with six violenns', which was one ahead of the Earl of Leicester, whose effects at Kenilworth in 1583 included 'a chest of five violens'.

The confusion of terminology regarding viols and violins is borne out by two pieces of evidence, the Lord Chamberlain's Accounts of the English court in the mid-sixteenth century, and the amusing travelogue published by Thomas Coryate in 1611 as *Crudities, hastily gobbled up in Five Month's Travel.* In 1547 an account for liveries of musicians at the funeral ceremonies of Henry VIII mentions Albertt de Venyce, Ambrose de Myllan, Marcke Anthonye, Frauncis de Vyzenza, Zorzi de Cremona and Vizenzo de Venetia as players of the vyolls, while Piero Wylder and Hans Aseneste

213

are listed as 'vyalls'. Eight years later, in a warrant for liveries dated 7 December 1555, Albert de Venice, Ambrose de Myllayne, Mark Anthonie, Frauncis de Venice, George de Cremona and Pawle Gayerdell (Paolo Gagliardello) are listed as 'violons', with Piro Wilder and Innocente de Comas as 'vialls'. Bearing in mind the differences in spelling of proper names and cities, and the confusion between Vicenza and Venice, it might also be possible to attribute to scribal error the appearance of two slightly different words, viols and violins. But there is also the possibility that the 1547 document intended 'violls' as an abbreviation for 'violl[in]s'. A third explanation would be that the sextet from northern Italy played both kinds of instrument according to the type of music required – viols for soothing fantasias, and violins for dances. Documents from 1556 onwards mention them again as viol-players.

Coryate's descriptions of music in Venice rank as some of the best on record. He was a lively, sharp-eared, witty observer whose comments offer abundant evidence of a considerable knowledge of music both vocal and instrumental. He mentions stringed instruments more than once in his account of the music at the basilica of San Marco and the Scoula di San Rocco, and by a strange coincidence he heard the same special kind of 'treble violl' in both places. Regarding his visit in 1608 he writes: 'At that time I heard much good musicke in Saint Markes Church, but especially that of a treble violl which was so excellent, that I thinke no man could surpasse it.' It is a well-known fact that Venetian musicians then, in the same way as musicians in the big cities of today, would so arrange their schedule of appearances that they might be seen and heard in neighbouring buildings, in different ensembles, two or three times in the same day. Is it possible that this outstanding performer on the treble viol also filled in at San Rocco? Of the feast in honour of that saint, Coryate writes: 'Of these treble violls I heard three several there, whereof each was so good, especially one that I observed above the rest, that I never heard the like before.' It is surely possible that this 'excellent treble viol' was in fact a violin, which by reason of its stronger tone stood out above the others. Violins were common in Venice at that time, but Coryate, coming as he did from a small village in England, may not have been sure of the difference between a viol and a violin.

In France violins were given a place of honour in the lavish court ballets which took place in the second half of the century. The *Ballet polonais* performed in August of 1573 enabled the Queen Mother, Catherine de' Medici, to impress members of the Polish Embassy with French dancing, costumes, music and magnificence, although the violinists were mostly Italians under the leadership of Belgiojoso, otherwise known as Balthasar de Beaujoyeux. On this occasion some thirty violins, presumably of different sizes and compasses, played (among other things) 'a very pleasing kind of warlike tune'. Even more famous and much more expensive than the *Ballet polonais* was the choreographic high point in the festivities accompanying the marriage of the Duc de Joyeuse and Mademoiselle de Vaudemont in 1581 – *Circe, ou le ballet comique de la reine*, published in the following year. Beaujoyeux, like Lully a century later (and another Italian violinist turned French), supervised not only the musical aspect of the production but also the ballet, and it may well have been because of this close link between music and dancing that the outcome was so successful. Not all the music was published, but the printed volume containing an elaborate account of the entertainment does provide examples of music for string orchestra: four pieces scored for violins 1 and 2, violas 1 and 2, cello (possibly doubled by bass as in later times), and one piece for twelve instruments. Although nothing in the uppermost part strikes one as being violinistically idiomatic, this music does rank as the first printed material in France that was genuinely intended for performance by violins.

Instruction books

Unfortunately there are no Renaissance treatises dealing

215

exclusively with the violin. Its role in music and in society was ill-defined for many years, and there was no call for such a treatise. One should not, however, underestimate the importance of the various general books of instruction, including those devoted ostensibly to ornamentation and embellishment, for it is frequently made clear in the prefaces that bowed instruments of the violin type could be employed just as well as other wind and string instruments.

In Brescia, one of the noted Italian centres of violin-making, instruments of the rebeck type are mentioned as early as 1533 by Giovanni Maria Lanfranco, whose main interests appear to have been theology, music and choirboys. The lively sparks of his musical imagination brought forth a theoretical work entitled *Scintille de musica*, one section of which describes in some detail the '*violette de arco senza tasti*', or 'little viols without frets, played with a bow'. These were instruments not far removed from the family of '*kleine Geigen*' or '*polnische Geigen*' discussed earlier. The Italian version had a pear-shaped body, and either four strings or (for the smallest) only three, always tuned in fifths. Zacconi, in his *Prattica di musica* (1592), tells us that Lanfranco's treatise describes '*violini*' although this word occurs nowhere in the Brescian publication. The terms '*violino*' and '*ribecchino*' were in fact to some extent interchangeable, as may be seen in Cerone's *El Melopeo y Maestro* (1613).

Andrea Gritti, the musically-inclined Doge who was largely responsible for Willaert's appointment at St Mark's, is named as the dedicatee of an instruction book for the recorder published at Venice in 1535 by Sylvestro di Ganassi. The title-page, however, makes it clear that the section dealing with ornamentation can just as easily be applied to other kinds of instruments – '*Utile ad ogni istrumento di fiato et chorde*'. It is possible that the rebeck players and violinists studying music in northern Italy about this time might have gleaned from this little volume a number of embellishments which sounded just as well on strings as on the recorder. But as far as fingering and bow technique were concerned, they had nothing to help them apart from personal tuition.

The 1530s seem to have been a critical period in the emergence of the violin, for it was in 1538 that the word '*violino*' first appeared (as far as we know) in an official document. The treasury records of Pope Paul III show that his considerable entourage at the peace conference at Nice in that year included numerous musicians, among them violinists from Milan. What kind of music they played is evident from the dispatches of the Venetian ambassador on July 14: 'The remainder of the day was taken up with feasting and dancing.'

Encouraged by the success of his publication of 1535, Ganassi followed it up by writing two books on the viol: *Regola Rubertina* (1542) dedicated (as is hinted by its title) to Roberto Strozzi, and its sequel, called *Lettione Seconda* (1543). His remarks on tuning are especially fascinating because of the reference to tuning by fifths – out of the question where the viols were concerned, but extremely useful when playing the '*viola da brazo senza tasti*,' by which he probably meant the type of nascent violin with three strings then being made by Andrea Amati. This matter was of such importance to Ganassi that he even mentioned it in the lengthy title of his 'second lesson', where the method of tuning the '*violone*' (viola da gamba) is said to be suitable also for those who play the '*viola senza tasti*'.

The problem with fretless instruments was – and still is – the daunting difficulty of perfect intonation. With hearing as the only guide to correct finger placement, almost everything depended upon the sensitivity of the player's ear and the speed with which his finger would react to a hair's breadth of faulty intonation. No wonder, Juan Bermudo stated in his *Declaracion de instrumentos* (1555), that the fretless vihuela was difficult to play in tune. He was not, of course, referring to a bowed string instrument, but the problem remained the same.

A composer of psalms, motets and Horatian odes, Philibert Jambe de Fer of Champlitte in Franche-Comté, wrote a short treatise on music which was published at Lyon in 1556. This *Épitome musical*, besides containing the rudiments of notation, offered its readers an introduction to the technique

217

and fingering of the cross-flute, the recorder, the viols and the violins, neatly contrasting two families of instruments whose individual members displayed considerable differences as well as similarities. In approaching his discussion of the violin, the author draws our attention to one similarity: both viols and violins tend to sound better when played in a key such as G, with one sharp in the signature, than in F or B flat. Mozart and Paganini, among others, used this idea to good effect when they composed works in which the solo part was written out in D (with a profusion of open strings) while the orchestra played in E flat. Bitonality was, of course, avoided by tuning the violin half-a-tone higher in order to give it even greater brilliance of sound.

Dissimilarities listed by Jambe de Fer include the viol's tuning in fourths and the 'sweeter' fifths used for the violin, the smaller body and harsher sound of the violin, its lack of frets, and the fact that the fingers of the left hand almost touched one another when playing consecutive notes. The four members of the family – *dessus*, *haute-contre*, *taille* and *bas* – tune by means of a unison G, and there is no real difference in technique between the Italian and the French school. Viols are played by gentlemen and merchants, whereas the violin (called in Italy *violon da braccia* or *violone*) is used for dancing, for which it is well suited by reason of its easy tuning, its portability and the advantage that it can be played while moving about.

He adds that the viols are played between the legs, or resting on a small stool, while the violins are held high, and on the arm ('da braccia') with a scarf or string attaching it securely to the performer's neck. The bass of the clan, or what we would call cello, was held even more securely by means of a hook and an iron ring. This could also be played while walking along, as can be seen from an illustration in Grewembroch's *Abiti e costumi veneziani*. This brief account of the violin family concludes with a somewhat deprecatory piece of advice – it is not worth illustrating, because few people play it, let alone live by it. The age of the session boys was yet to dawn.

By 1584 players of viols and violins could purchase a book on embellishment and variations by the head of the Venetian wind-band, Girolamo dalla Casa: *Il vero modo di diminuir . . . Libro secondo.* The first volume, identical in title, concerned itself rather more with wind instruments, whereas the second mentioned in its prefatory remarks that singers could perform the various chansons and madrigals along with all kinds of instruments – '*viole da gamba, e viole da brazzo*'. Just a year later, in 1585, another musician in the service of the Doge compiled a collection of *Ricercate, Passaggi, et Cadentie* for the use of players on all kinds of wind instruments as well as the viola – he does not specify which one of the species, but probably intended to include both. A similarly all-embracing figure of speech is employed by Giovanni Luca Conforto in the expansive title of his *Breve e facile maniera* . . . of 1593.

The player who could teach himself how to rattle off these fancy cadences, rhetorical flourishes and deft divisions stood an excellent chance of becoming a virtuoso of high renown, despite the pessimistic view of the gentleman from Lyon less than half-a-century before. If the violin took root as a musical instrument of value and purpose in the middle of the century, it certainly came into its own in the last two decades, fore-armed thanks to its four strings in readiness for the slow but irreversible struggle from which it emerged the undisputed victor by the end of the seventeenth century. The viols vanished almost from the sight and sound of man until they were revived in the late Victorian era, but the violin went on from strength to length, increasing the span of its neck and the thickness of its bass-bar, improving its sound, even influencing the shape and design of the magic wand by whose means a ravishing sound could be conjured forth.

A widening and seemingly endless road opened up for the violin as the age of the 'basso continuo' dawned. It could hold its own as a solo instrument supported by lute, harpsichord or organ; it sounded even better when a second violin was added and the trio-sonata came into its own, and when (on rare occasions) three violins were heard playing separate parts, as in certain works by Purcell, Telemann, Handel and Pachelbel, an almost pyrotechnical brilliance dominated the scene. Scordatura, or deliberate mis-tuning of the strings, enabled virtuosi such as Biber and Vivaldi to produce effects of unimaginable subtlety and sonority, while the tonal advances made by the great *luthiers* of Cremona provided the violin with a carrying power that cried out for the invention of the concerto. Torelli and Vivaldi obliged, and the rest of the musical world followed suit. The German school developed double-stopping, but there was no stopping the violin: it had been well and truly launched on a career of magnificent promise and proportions. As a solo instrument, in chamber music, and in orchestras, it was to create and maintain a position of influence and of importance. The fiddler became the violinist.

Thirteen

Bach's Sonatas and Partitas for Violin*

A monumental challenge to violinists for over two hundred and fifty years, Bach's 'Six Solos for Violin without Bass Accompaniment' – as he described them on the cover of his autograph – happily show no signs of age and offer no hint whatever that their quasi-hypnotic sway over players and public will ever diminish. The reason is not hard to seek. Such music, and by such a master, would command and rivet attention no matter how it might be scored; but scored as it is for an instrument with but four strings (and the smallest member of its family at that), this set of sonatas and partitas calls for a mastery of technique and a gift of sheer virtuosity the like of which had never been known before Bach's time, and has rarely been exceeded since. The art of writing for an unaccompanied violin nevertheless enjoys a long and fascinating history, of which a brief summary may not be out of place.

Polyphony on the Violin before Bach. It lies in the physical nature of the violin and its bow that, from time to time at least, more than one note – either a double-stop or a chord – ought to emerge, if only by accident. Too flat a bridge will produce such accidents automatically, and since illustrations of medieval fiddles often show a flattish bridge, it may be that minstrels made a much more extensive use of multiple-stops than is usually acknowledged. In the 1560s, the madrigalist and virtuoso on the viola da braccio Alessandro Striggio (father of the Mantuan court secretary who wrote the

---

*No section on the history of the violin and its music would be complete without an analysis of these seminal works.

libretto for Monteverdi's *Orfeo*) was said to have delighted listeners by playing *four parts* simultaneously, and even if he was using a lira da braccio – which had more strings than a viola da braccio – his dexterity must have been of an entirely unusual nature.

Nothing remotely approaching Striggio's feat can be found in later Italian violin music, and it seems that only Nicola Matteis achieved comparable artistic results when he settled in London about the year 1672, publishing soon afterwards various books of solos 'with full stops for the Violin'. He had been preceded in 1656 by a German virtuoso from Lübeck, Thomas Baltzer, whose chord-playing and polyphony astonished the connoisseurs of London, Oxford, and Cambridge. If those same connoisseurs could have travelled to Germany, they would have found even more remarkable talent among violinists, especially in such men as Johann Schmelzer, Clemens Thieme, Nathan Schnittelbach, Johann Furchheim, and Nicholaus Strungk. But the rapid strides in violin technique at that time were due to two men in particular, one of them the son of a gamekeeper, the other a valet to a Polish nobleman – Heinrich Biber (1644–1704), and Johann Jakob Walther (1650–1717). Although at the time by far the most important aspect of Biber's career was his work as director of music at Salzburg cathedral, it was his chamber music and violin sonatas that set the seal of fame upon his reputation abroad. The last of those sonatas is a Passacaglia for violin alone, a work of outstanding interest by reason of its brilliance, resource, and sonority, and a worthy forerunner of Bach's great Chaconne.

Walther, like Biber, made extensive use of the deliberate mis-tuning of violin strings known as *scordatura*, which permitted effects and bariolage of a sometimes startling kind. A countryman and contemporary of theirs, Daniel Eberlin, once calculated that there were 2,000 possible ways of tuning a violin, although history does not record his ever having committed those calculations to paper. Indeed, he need not have done so, for the entire German school of violinists took up the idea and even managed to tempt the Italians,

Plate 21. Minstrel (right) playing medieval fiddle

ho dicūr et potencōr Creso et augūo

21

trocinio confidentez.
perpetua defensione
conserua. Oratio.
Mnes sancti
tui quesum
dne nos ubi
qʒ adiuuent. ut dū
eorum merita recoli
mus patrocinia sen
tiamus. Et pacem tu
am nostris concede

22

one of whom – Vivaldi – went so far as to write concertos for a violin tuned to b-d-a-d, or a-e-a-e. Walther, in his published collections of solos, named *Hortulus chelicus* and *Scherzi da Violino Solo*, explores every conceivable effect of bowing and fingering besides demonstrating an uncommon mastery of polyphonic violin writing.

Nicolaus Bruhns, the town organist of Husum, achieved considerable fame in spite of his regrettably short life (1665–97), for apart from the excellence of his choral compositions and organ music he extracted unrivalled sonorities from his violin, which he played on the organ bench while adding a bass part on the pedals. Equally gifted, though in a different way, was the Dresden-born violinist Johann Paul von Westhoff (1656–1705), who capped a career as virtuoso violinist by becoming professor of languages at the University of Wittenberg. In his heyday Westhoff played before the monarchy and nobility of all Europe, his finest hour being a recital for Louis XIV, who warmly approved of a sonata and a suite (the latter for unaccompanied violin), both of which were published in Paris without delay. The Suite in A makes extensive use of double-stops, chords, and contrapuntal writing, the total impression being one of extraordinary inventiveness.

These men were the most noteworthy of Bach's predecessors in the field of unaccompanied violin music. That he easily surpassed their efforts goes without saying, but it is less well known that the tradition continued to flourish both in Germany and elsewhere. Telemann wrote a set of twelve fantasias for violin without accompaniment in 1735, when the Swede J. H. Roman was engaged in producing his *Assaggi per Violino Solo*. Many years later the French composer Louis-Gabriel Guillemain devoted an entire collection (his Op. 18 of 1762) to what he chose to call *Amusements pour le Violon*.

Bach as a Violinist. No contemporaneous descriptions of Bach's violin-playing survive. Thanks to Johann Nicolaus Forkel, however, an account of the master's life-long pre-

Plate 22. Lower right: early Renaissance fiddle   223

occupation with the violin survives in a letter from C. P. E. Bach, whom Forkel knew and corresponded with when he first began to collect materials for his essay on Bach. In 1774 C. P. E. Bach included the following words in a letter to the 25-year-old musicologist: 'As the greatest expert and judge of harmony [J. S. Bach] liked best to play the viola, with appropriate loudness and softness. In his youth, and until the approach of old age, he played the violin cleanly and penetratingly, and thus kept the orchestra in better order than he could have done with the harpsichord. He understood to perfection the possibilities of all stringed instruments. This is evidenced by his solos for the violin and for the violoncello without bass. One of the greatest violinists told me once that he had seen nothing more perfect for learning to be a good violinist, and could suggest nothing better to anyone eager to learn, than the said violin solos without bass'.

Who was the virtuoso responsible for this prophetic statement? In all probability, it was Friedrich Wilhelm Rust (1739–96), a student of both Friedemann and C. P. E. Bach, and as fine a harpsichordist as he was a violinist. Rust's elder brother had played in old Bach's orchestra, and his grandson Wilhelm Rust (1822–92) was to become one of the editors of the Bach-Gesellschaft. More than this, and surely more than a coincidence, is the fact that Rust owned towards the end of his life the only true autograph of the Sonatas and Partitas, which he had acquired from a member of the Bach family – Christina Louisa of Bückeburg. This brings us to the important question of source-materials, authentic and otherwise.

The Sources of Bach's Sonatas and Partitas. When Alfred Dörffel edited the works for unaccompanied violin and violoncello for the Bach-Gesellschaft (prefatory material dated 1879) he knew only three manuscripts and three printed editions. Manuscript *A* was considered to be either an autograph of Bach or of his second wife Anna Magdalena, whose handwriting closely resembled his. A note in the hand of Georg Pölschau states that it was found in a pile of old music about to be used as wrapping-paper in St. Petersburg. The manuscript was in a far from perfect state, the D minor Partita having at some time been torn out and replaced by a later copy on paper of a different format. Dörffel's second source, Manuscript *B*, also came from the Pölschau collection, at that time in the Royal Library of Berlin, and it too rated as a Bach autograph from his Leipzig period. Manuscript *C*, a copy made by Bach's pupil Johann Peter Kellner, proved to be of considerable use in the establishment of a plausible text, in spite of the fact that the B minor Partita was missing from the set.

As his printed sources, Dörffel listed the edition of 1802 (Simrock, Bonn); the second edition, dated 1843 (Kistner, Leipzig); and lastly Schumann's reprint with piano accompaniment which appeared first in six books in 1854 (Breitkopf und Härtel, Leipzig), then somewhat later as a double volume – score and violin part. None of these were based on the unique autograph, which still belonged at that time to the Bach family. It was first used as the basis of a practical edition by Joseph Joachim, who consulted it in or before 1909 at the house of Dr Erich Prieger in Bonn. At a later date it was acquired by the Prussian State Library (MS number P.967), and on the dispersal of that collection during World War II it found its way, together with a considerable number of Bach autographs, to the University of Tübingen. A very good facsimile was published by Insel–Verlag, Leipzig (1958), with a preface by Yehudi Menuhin and a commentary by Günter Hausswald.

How did such a precious autograph remain unknown to the Bach scholars of the nineteenth century? Spitta certainly never saw it; but on the other hand it was known to Brahms, who may have heard about it from Joachim. Presumably the manuscript passed into the possession of Anna Magdalena on the death of her husband, and then came into the hands of Johann Christoph Friedrich Bach (1732–95), her ninth child. But it is also possible that he received it as a gift from his father when he left the family circle to go and practise his art in Bückeburg. What use, if any, he made of it is not known. The inscription 'Louisa Bach, Bückeburg, 1842' suggests that she, one of the daughters of J. C. F. Bach, added it to her library in that year, when she was eighty years old. But it could not have come directly from her father, and the probable explanation is that she inherited it from her elder brother, Wilhelm Friedrich Ernst (1759–1845), cembalist to Queen Louisa and last of the male descendants of Johann Sebastian Bach.

Whatever its history and adventures, the manuscript possesses an intrinsic value almost beyond estimation. Here, in the flowing, clear, and compelling hand of the master, is a vivid record of a great organist's attempt to coax from the violin – by means of harmonic suggestion, contrapuntal ingenuity, or sonorous chords – the kind of textural cornucopia that he knew and loved so well. One of his own sons testified to his skill as a violinist, but we must inevitably feel that he was sometimes frustrated by the limitations of such an instrument. He owned an ordinary violin which was valued at 2 thalers, and a fine Jacob Stainer valued at 8 thalers. He played the Stainer when he led the orchestra, and meditated musically upon it when, in 1720, he wrote down the Sonatas and Partitas in their final form. He succeeded in fusing together the basically Italianate forms of chamber or church sonata with the grandiloquent polyphony of the German violin school, and if there is more of the organ in these six superb compositions than one finds in the works of Biber, Walther, or Westhoff, the modern interpreter and his audience have all the more reason to rejoice.

Schering and Schweitzer, both convinced that Bach's chords could only be properly played with a bow whose hair was capable of being slackened and tightened by the thumb of the player, unwittingly helped to bring into the world a so-called Bach bow which was totally unknown to Bach and foreign to his principles. This twentieth-century invention could indeed play on all four strings simultaneously, but it lacked the agility to cope with the more brilliant and intricate passage-work in the fugues and *doubles*. As Dr Beckmann pointed out in his pioneering treatise of 1918 (*Das Violinspiel in Deutschland vor 1700*), the correct solution can be found only by studying Bach's notation. Like lute tablature, it is liable to widely differing interpretations, the right one lying approximately half-way between the extremes adopted by deservedly discredited fanatics. Many generations of violinists owe thanks to Ferdinand David for including the text of manuscript *A* on a separate stave below his edited version, issued in 1843 for the benefit of students at the Leipzig Conservatorium, and to Joseph Joachim for following the same procedure in his edition of 1909. At least some part of Bach's pristine musical thought has always been available, and whatever divergences may appear in performances today, it is certain that scholarship and common-sense will prevail over mere quirks of fashion.

The Sonatas and Partitas

Sonata No. 1 (G minor) 1: *Adagio.* A slow harmonic rhythm remains in perfect balance with mobile and flowing fioriture, linking the richly expressive chords in leisurely and meditative fashion. 2: *Fuga – Allegro.* Arranged by Bach for organ, and by an unknown transcriber for lute, this fugue nevertheless sounds best on the violin, to which the epigrammatic subject is perfectly suited. Passages of dense yet highly effective counterpoint alternate with episodes in which arpeggio formulae suggest with ease and power a modulation scheme which only Bach could devise. 3: *Siciliana.* What was once a lively dance appears now as a relaxed, persuasive melody beautified by harmonic comments and filigree decoration, the key being B flat major. 4: *Presto.* This is the first of Bach's movements (and there are many more to come) in the style of a *moto perpetuo* – a certain basic note-value, once chosen, persists right to the end of the movement, the total impression being one of dazzling brilliance and inexhaustible energy.

Partita No. 1 (B minor) 1: *Allemanda & Double.* The somewhat stiff and jerky thrust of this old German dance is toned down

227

from time to time by an unruffled triplet figure, and when the double (or variation) follows, the mood is even more smooth and quiet. 2: *Corrente & Double*. The perpetual motion in the main dance is in eighth-notes, whose bold leaps paint in the harmony; but in the variation, marked *Presto*, sixteenth-notes predominate and the pace becomes breathless and challenging. 3: *Sarabande*. Chordal writing prevails in this slow and stately version of a once lascivious dance, and the variation relies upon triplet figures throughout. 4: *Tempo di Borea*. A vigorous dance in 4/4 time, with the downbeats emphasized by four-note chords. The double also makes use of double-stops here and there, but its movement in the main is constant and consistently in eighth-notes.

Sonata No. 2 (A minor) 1: *Grave*. Like the prelude to the first sonata, this one suggests solemn and slow-moving harmonies supporting a festoon of delicate ornament, the improvisatory element always being in evidence. 2: *Fuga*. Bach arranged this for keyboard, down a fifth. Of the pithy subject, a contemporary of Bach's, Johann Mattheson, wrote: 'Who would ever think that these eight short notes could be fruitful enough to give rise naturally to a counterpoint of more than a whole sheet of music without any considerable extension? And yet this has been done, as is plainly to be seen, by the great Bach of Leipzig, who was particularly happy in this kind of composition; and more than that, it is treated directly and in inversion'. 3: *Andante*. A duet, in effect, for one violin, with a singing melody above supported by a non-contrapuntal bass. 4: *Allegro*. Dactylic figures pepper this lively finale, in which Bach has been careful to note sudden changes from loud to soft.

Partita No. 2 (D minor) 1: *Allemanda*. Less spiky than the B minor Allemanda, this one nevertheless includes some of those smoother triplet figures which characterize Bach's compositions in this dance-style. There is no variation to this or any other dance in the present Partita. 2: *Corrente*. Triplet figures and smooth runs predominate, varied by dotted-note patterns and occasional chords. 3: *Sarabanda*. Expressive and dignified, yet rich in harmonic colour and modulation. 4: *Gigue*. Each half begins as a gigue should, but soon shifts into a *moto perpetuo* mood in which sequences play an important role. 5: *Ciaccona*. A gigantic creation formed from the humblest of Renaissance bass-patterns. In terms of sheer resource, harmonic impetus, and polyphonic bravura, Bach set a standard that has never been approached, leave alone matched or surpassed.

Sonata No. 3 (C major) 1: *Adagio*. Its character derives from the inexorable dotted-note figure, only rarely broken up by cadenza-like interludes. Bach arranged this movement for keyboard, transposing it to G major. 2: *Fuga*. Longer than the other fugue subjects, this one bears more than a passing resemblance to the melody of 'Komm heiliger Geist'. It is a noble and sustained piece of polyphony, in which the subject is developed in its inverted form as well as right way up. 3. *Largo*. In arioso style: the accompaniment is generally simple and unobtrusive, as befits a work of Italianate allure. 4: *Allegro assai*. Another breathtaking finale, combining bariolage with rapid runs within an apparently endless flow of harmonic invention.

Partita No. 3 (E major) 1: *Preludio*. This scintillating movement, put down a tone to D, was used in Bach's Cantata No. 29 ('Wir danken dir, Gott') for the election of the Leipzig town council in 1731. 2: *Louré*. A lilting movement in 6/4 time, mostly in duet style though with some chords at climactic points. 3: *Gavotte en Rondeaux*. Bach's endearing use of plural suggests that he wished to point up the frequent re-statements of a theme which ranks among his best known. 4: *Menuet*. The first minuet forms the outer arches of this tripartite structure, while the second, in central position, offers contrast through its cunning use of an inverted drone. 5: *Bourreé*. A fast movement in duple time, rich in dynamic contrasts. 6: *Gigue*. A graceful ending to a partita of exceptional beauty and variety.

Brief Glossary*

Détaché: A smooth stroke, the bow drawing the sound without leaving the string; the bow changes inaudible at all speeds and all volumes. This is the violinist's basic stroke.

Flautato: A whispering sound produced by drawing the bow without pressure (using only its own weight) and with a certain speed.

Legato: A form of détaché in which many notes are played on one stroke, 'legato' meaning 'bound' or 'tied with one another'.

Martelé: Energetic, fast and brief strokes, usually played in the upper half of the bow, though they can be done in the lower half as well, and are in fact a most excellent exercise when done in the lower as well as the upper half.

Pizzicato: This is a plucking of the string; when done with the right hand it produces a banjo- or guitar-like effect. It can also be produced with the left-hand fingers. It is only possible to pluck a note with the finger placed above that note; therefore no ascending scales would be possible, only descending.

Ponticello (on the bridge): A stroke in which the bow is drawn very near the bridge, where the bow does not achieve sufficient grip on the string to make it oscillate properly, the string

*See also pp. 62-79.

231

being too resistant at its extremity. This produces a whistling and eerie sound.

Spiccato: A short bouncing stroke, using the elasticity of the bow-stroke, the bow-hair and the string, which enables the bow to leave the string between each stroke. This is played usually in the middle of the bow and in the lower half when louder and slower.

Staccato: A stroke in which each note is separated from the previous and succeeding ones, and which can be played at great speed up- or down-bow, sounding like a succession of martelés. *Flying Staccato:* A variant in which the bow leaves the string between each note.

Sul tasto (on the finger-board): This gives a velvety and cooing sound. The string is soft, not as resistant, and cannot take any pressure.

Some selected further reading

The Viola: The Complete Guide for Teacher and Student, by Henry Barrett (University of Alabama Press).
Basic String Repairs, by Arthur Burgan (Oxford University Press).
Violin Teaching in Class, by Gertrude Collins (Oxford University Press, 1962).
Violin: Six Lessons with Yehudi Menuhin, by Yehudi Menuhin (Faber, 1971).
The Teaching of Action in String Playing, by Paul Rolland and Marla Mutschler (University of Illinois Press).
Simplicity of Playing the Violin, by Herbert Whone (Gollancz, 1972).

Some selected exercises

Flesch: Urstudien; Kierman: Practising the Violin, Practising the Viola; Sladek: Thirty Minutes a Day; Dounis: The Daily Dozen, The Artist's Technique of Violin Playing; Sevcic: The Violin School for Beginners, The School for Violin Technique for Advanced Students.

Etudes (Gaviniés, Rodé, Mazas, etc.); Caprices (Paganini, Sauret etc.).

Discography

Some Selected Violin Records

Any short list of records must necessarily be highly selective. Moreover any selection is governed by the availability of records at any given time. Nearly but not all of the records listed here were available at the time of going to press; some will no doubt disappear from circulation; others that have disappeared will, one hopes, return on other labels. The list has glaring omissions but it is designed to give the reader starting to collect records some rough guidance in starting to build up a library of violin records for himself.
(R.L.)

BACH, Johann Sebastian
(1685–1750)
Concerto in A minor, BWV1041
Concerto in E major, BWV1042
David Oistrakh, Vienna Symphony
DG138820
Melkus, Vienna Capella Academica
DG2533 075
Zukerman, English Chamber
Orchestra   CBS 72964
Harnoncourt, Vienna Concentus
Musicus   SAWT9508
Menuhin, Robert Masters Chamber
Orchestra   HMV ASD346
Menuhin, Orchestre Symphonique
de Paris/Enesco (rec. 1936 and 33)
HMV COLH 77*
Concerto in D minor for two violins
and strings, BWV1043
David and Igor Oistrakh, RPO/
Goossens   DG138820
Melkus, Rantos, Vienna Capella
Academica   DG2533 075
Zukerman, Perlman, ECO/
Barenboim   HMV ASD2783

Harnoncourt, Pfeiffer, Vienna
Concentus Musicus   SAWT9508
Ayo, Michelucci, I Musici
Philips 6580 021
Grumiaux, Toyoda, New
Philharmonia/de Waart
Philips 6500 119
Menuhin, Ferras, Robert Masters
Chamber Orchestra   HMV ASD346
Menuhin, Enesco, Orchestre
Symphonique/Monteux
HMV COLH 77*
Concerto for violin, oboe and strings,
BWV1060
Grumiaux, Holliger, New
Philharmonia/de Waart
Philips 6500 119
Menuhin, Goossens, Bath Festival
Orchestra   HMV ASD500
Brandenburg Concertos 1–6,
BWV1046–51
Philomusica/Thurston Dart
Oiseau Lyre SOL60005–6
Vienna Concentus Musicus/
Harnoncourt   SAWT9459–60

* denotes not currently available in the UK

235

Violin and Viola

English Chamber Orchestra/
Britten   Decca SET410–11
Collegium Aureum
                BASF BAC3007–8
Würtemberg Chamber Orchestra/
Faerber   Turnabout TV3044–45S
Bath Festival Orchestra/Menuhin
        HMV ASD327–8 (or SLS831)
Six Sonatas for violin and clavier,
BMV1014–9
Frydén, Leonhardt   SAWT9433–4
Szeryng, Walcha   Philips 6700 017
Schneiderhan, Karl Richter
                        DG2722 012
Oistrakh, Pischner   DG2726 002
Partitas and Sonatas for solo violin,
BWV1001–6
Heifetz   RCA SER5669–71
Menuhin HMV ALP1512, 1531–2*
Grumiaux   Philips SAL3472–4
Szeryng   DG2709 028
Suk   HMV SLS828
Milstein   DG2709 047

BARBER, Samuel (b 1910)
Violin Concerto (1940)
Stern, New York Philharmonic/
Bernstein   CBS 61621

BARTÓK, Bela (1881–1945)
Concerto No. 1 (1908 pub. 1958)
Viola Concerto (1945 ed. Serly)
Menuhin, New Philharmonia/Dorati
                HMV ASD2323*
Violin Concerto No. 2 (1938)
Szeryng, Concertgebouw Orchestra/
Haitink   Philips 6500 021
Szekely, Concertgebouw Orchestra/
Mengelberg
(rec. 1939 fp)   Qualiton LPX11573
Perlman, LSO/Previn
                HMV ASD3014
Menuhin, New Philharmonia/Dorati
                HMV ASD2281*
Two Portraits (1908)
(No. 1 identical with Violin Concerto
No. 1 first movement)
Szigeti, Philharmonia Orchestra/
Lambert   HMV HLM7016
Röhn, Frankfurt Radio Orchestra/
Inbal   Philips 6500 781
Two Rhapsodies for violin and
orchestra
Menuhin, BBC Symphony
Orchestra/Boulez   HMV ASD2449
Szeryng, Concertgebouw Orchestra/
Haitink   Philips 6500 021
Sonata No. 1 for violin and piano
(1921)
André Gertler, Diane Andersen
            Supraphon SUAST 50650

Stern, Zakin   CBS 73117
Yehudi and Hephzibah Menuhin
                HMV ALP1705*
Sonata No. 2 for violin and piano
(1922)
Stern, Zakin   CBS 73117
Gertler, Andersen
            Supraphon SUAST 50481
Forty-four Duos for two violins (1931)
Gertler, Suk
            Supraphon SUAST 50770
6 only: Menuhin, Gotkovsky
                HMV ASD2281*
Sonata for solo violin (1944)
(dedicated to Yehudi Menuhin)
Menuhin   HMV ALP1705*
Gertler   Supraphon SUAST50481

BEETHOVEN, Ludwig van
(1770–1827)
Violin Concerto in D major, Op. 61
David Oistrakh, ORTF Orchestra/
Cluytens   HMV SXLP30168
Kulenkampff, Berlin Philharmonic/
Schmidt-Isserstedt (rec. 1936)
                Telefunken KT11008
Heifetz, NBC Symphony/Toscanini
                RCA DPS2006
Suk, New Philharmonia/Boult
                HMV ASD2667
Grumiaux, New Philharmonia/
Galliera   Philips SAL3616
Grumiaux, Concertgebouw/Davis
                Philips 6500 775
Szeryng, Concertgebouw/Haitink
                Philips 6500 531
Ferras, Berlin Philharmonic/Karajan
                DG139021
Menuhin, New Philharmonia/
Klemperer   HMV ASD2285
Romances for violin and orchestra
Heifetz, RCA Symphony Orchestra/
Steinberg   RCA DPS2006
David Oistrakh, RPO/Goossens
                DG138714
Grumiaux, New Philharmonia/de
Waart   6580 047
Szeryng, Concertgebouw/Haitink
                Philips 6500 137
Menuhin, Philharmonia/Furtwängler
(rec. 1953)   HMV HLM7015
Violin Sonatas (complete)
Zukerman, Barenboim
                HMV SLS871
Menuhin, Kempff   DG2735 001
Szigeti, Arrau (rec. 1944)
                RCA SRV300–3
Sonatas Op. 12, Nos. 1–3
Grumiaux, Haskil Philips 6580 090
Sonata in F, Op. 24 ('Spring')
Grumiaux, Haskil Philips 6580 032

Oistrakh, Oborin   Philips SAL3420
Szeryng, Rubinstein
                    RCA SER5701-3
Yehudi and Hephzibah Menuhin
                    HMV SXLP30164
Sonata in C minor, Op. 30, No. 2
Oistrakh, Oborin   Philips SAL3418
Sonata in G major, Op. 30, No. 3
Szeryng, Rubinstein
                    RCA SER5701-3
Kreisler, Rachmaninoff
                    RCA VIC6059
Oistrakh, Oborin   SAL3416
Menuhin, Kempff   ·DG2530 135
Sonata in A, Op. 47 ('Kreutzer')
Grumiaux, Haskil   Philips 6580 032
Heifetz, Smith   RCA DPS2006
Oistrakh, Oborin   Philips SAL3419
Perlman, Ashkenazy
                    Decca SXL6632
Yehudi and Hephzibah Menuhin
                    HMV SXLP30164
Menuhin, Kempff   DG2530 135
Sonata in G major, Op. 96
Oistrakh, Oborin   Philips SAL3417

BERG, Alban (1885–1935)
Violin Concerto (1935)
Menuhin, BBC Symphony
Orchestra/Boulez   HMV ASD2449

BERKELEY, Lennox (b 1903)
Violin Concerto, Op. 59 (1961)
(dedicated to Yehudi Menuhin)
Menuhin, Menuhin Festival
Orchestra/Boult   HMV ASD2759

BERLIOZ, Hector (1803–69)
Reverie et Caprice, Op. 8 (1839)
Rosand, Südwestdeutscher
Rundfunks Orchestra/Reinhardt
                Turnabout TV34466S
Grumiaux, New Philharmonia/de
Waart   Philips 6580 047
Harold in Italy, Op. 16 (1834)
Cooley, NBC Symphony/Toscanini
                    RCA AT112
Primrose, Boston SO/Münch
                    RCA VICS1580
Lincer, New York Philharmonic/
Bernstein   CBS 61091
Menuhin, Philharmonia Orchestra/
Davis   HMV ASD537

BLISS, Arthur (1891–1975)
Violin Concerto
Campoli, LPO/Bliss Decca ACL317

BLOCH, Ernest (1880–1959)
Violin Concerto (1938)
Menuhin, Philharmonia Orchestra/
Kletzki   HMV SXLP30177

BRAHMS, Johannes (1833–97)
Violin Concerto in D, Op. 77
Heifetz, Boston Symphony/Münch
                    RCA DPS2002
Menuhin, Lucerne Festival
Orchestra/Furtwängler
                    HMV HLM7015
Kogan, Philharmonia Orchestra/
Kondrashin   HMV SXLP30063
Kreisler, LPO/Barbirolli (rec. 1936)
            World Record Club SH115
David Oistrakh, Cleveland
Orchestra/Szell   HMV ASD2525
Grumiaux, New Philharmonia/Davis
                    Philips 6500 299
Szeryng, Concertgebouw/Haitink
                    Philips 6500 530
Krebbers, Concertgebouw/Haitink
                    Philips 6580 087
Concerto for violin and cello and
orchestra Op. 102
Mischakoff, Miller, NBC Symphony/
Toscanini   RCA AT125
Francescatti, Fournier, Columbia
SO/Walter   CBS S61428
Schneiderhan, Starker, RIAS/
Fricsay   DG2726 008
David Oistrakh, Rostropovich,
Cleveland/Szell   HMV SLS786
Campoli, Navarra, Hallé/Barbirolli
                    Pye GSGC14009
Violin Sonata in G, Op. 78
Suk, Katchen   Decca SXL6321
Szeryng, Rubinstein
                    RCA SER5701-3
Menuhin, Kentner HMV ASD474*
Violin Sonata in A, Op. 100
Suk, Katchen   Decca SXL6321
Szeryng, Rubinstein
                    RCA SER5701-3
Menuhin, Kentner HMV ASD474*
Violin Sonata in D minor, Op. 108
Suk, Katchen   Decca SXL6321
Szeryng, Rubinstein
                    RCA SER5701-3
Menuhin, Kentner HMV ASD475*
Oistrakh, Richter HMV ASD2618
Sonata in F minor for viola and piano,
Op. 120, No. 1
Sonata in E flat, Op. 120, No. 2
Kodusek, Novotny
                 Supraphon 111 1178

BRITTEN, Benjamin (b 1913)
Violin Concerto, Op. 13 (1939)
Lubotsky, ECO/Britten
                    Decca SXL6512

BRUCH, Max (1838–1920)
Violin Concerto No.1 in G minor, Op.26
Menuhin, Philarmonia/Süsskind
                    HMV ASD334

237

Violin and Viola

Heifetz, New Symphony/Sargent
RCA LSB4061
Grumiaux, Concertgebouw/Haitink
Philips 6580 022
Igor Oistrakh, RPO/David Oistrakh
DG135039
Kyung-Wha Chung, RPO/Kempe
Decca SXL6573
Perlman, LSO/Previn
HMV ASD2926
Fujikawa, Rotterdam Phil/de Waart
Philips 6500 708
Menuhin, LSA/Boult
HMV ASD2852
Violin Concerto No. 2 in D minor,
Op. 44
Menuhin, LSO/Boult
HMV ASD2852
Scottish Fantasy, Op. 46
David Oistrakh, LSO/Horenstein
Decca SXL6035
Kyung-Wha Chung, RPO/Kempe
Decca SXL6573
Heifetz, New Symphony/Sargent
RCA LSB4105

CHAUSSON, Ernest (1855–99)
'Poème' for violin and orchestra,
Op. 20
Milstein, Philharmonia/Fistoulari
HMV SXLP30159
Igor Oistrakh, Moscow Radio
Orchestra/Rozhdestvesnky
HMV ASD2813

CORELLI, Arcangelo (1653–1713)
Sonatas, Op. 5
Kovacs, Banda, Sebastian
Qualiton SLPX11514–5

DEBUSSY, Claude (1862–1918)
Violin Sonata in G minor (1917)
Stern, Zakin   CBS 73117
Oistrakh, Bauer   Philips SAL3589*
Grumiaux, Hajdu   Philips SAL3644*

DELIUS, Frederick (1862–1934)
Violin Concerto
Sammons, Liverpool Phil/Sargent
World Records SH224
Pougnet, RPO/Beecham
HMV ALP1890*
Violin Sonatas 1–3
Ralph Holmes, Eric Fenby
Unicorn RHS310

DVORÁK, Antonin (1841–1904)
Violin Concerto in A minor, Op. 53
Suk, Czech Philharmonic/Ancerl
Supraphon SUAST50181

Violin Sonata in F, Op. 57
Violin Sonatina in G, Op. 100
Four Romantic Pieces, Op. 75
Suk, Holacek
Supraphon 111 1312–3

ELGAR, Edward (1857–1934)
Violin Concerto in B minor, Op. 61
Sammons, New Queen's Hall
Orchestra/Wood (rec. 1928)
HMV HLM7011
Menuhin, LSO/Elgar (rec. 1932)
HMV ALP1456
Menuhin, NPO/Boult
HMV ASD2259
Heifetz, LSO/Sargent RCA LSB4022
Sonata in E minor, Op. 80
Bean, Parkhouse   HMV HQS1252
Sammons, Murdoch
Columbia LX379–81†
†for information only: LX379–81 are
in the process of being transferred to
LP.

ENESCO, Georges (1881–1955)
Violin Sonata No. 3 in A minor,
Op. 25
Yehudi and Hephzibah Menuhin
HMV ASD2294
Enesco, Lipatti   DLX40–41

FAURÉ, Gabriel (1845–1924)
Violin Sonata No. 1 in A, Op. 13
Thibaud, Cortot   HMV COLH 74*
Ferras, Barbizet   HMV CVA856*

FRANCK, César (1822–90)
Violin Sonata in A
Perlman, Ashkenazy
Decca SXL6408
Oistrakh, Richter   HMV ASD2618
Thibaud, Cortot   HMV COLH74*
Menuhin, Kentner   HMV BLP1082

GERHARD, Roberto (1896–1970)
Violin Concerto
Nyman, BBC Symphony/Davis
Argo ZRG701

GLAZUNOV, Alezander
(1865–1936)
Violin Concerto in A minor, Op. 82
Heifitz, RCA Symphony/Hendl
RCA LSB4061
Marcovici, LSO/Stokowski
Decca OPFS3–4

GRIEG, Edvard (1843–1907)
Violin Sonata in C minor, Op. 45
Gertler, Farnadi HMV SXLP20085
Kreisler, Rachmaninoff
RCA VICS6059

HANDEL, Georg Frideric
(1685–1759)
Concerti grossi Op. 6
St. Martin's Academy/Marriner
Decca SXL6369–71
Bath Festival/Menuhin
HMV ASD604, 598, 491*
ECO/Leppard Philips 6747 036
Sonatas Op. 1, Nos. 3, 10, 12–15
Menuhin, Malcolm, Gauntlett
HMV ASD2384*

HARRIS, Roy (b 1898)
Violin Sonata (1942)
Shapiro, Harris CCS S8012†
†Available in U.S. only.

HAYDN, Franz Joseph (1732–1809)
Violin Concerto in C, Hob VIIa/I
Grumiaux, ECO/Leppard
Philips SAL3489*

HENZE, Hans Werner (b 1926)
Violin Concerto No. 1 (1948)
Schneiderhan, Bayerisches
Rundfunks Orchestra/Henze
DG139382
*Violin Concerto No. 2, for tape, voices
and thirteen instruments*
Langbein, Sinfonietta/Henze
Decca HEAD5

HINDEMITH, Paul (1895–1963)
Violin Concerto (1939)
David Oistrakh, LSO/Hindemith
Decca SXL6035
Gertler, Czech Philharmonic/Ancerl
Supraphon 110 0508

KHACHATURYAN, Aram
(b 1903)
Violin Concerto (1940)
Kogan, Boston Symphony/Münch
RCA VICS1153
David Oistrakh, Philharmonia/
Khachaturyan Columbia 33CX1303

KORNGOLD, Erich (1897–1957)
Violin Concerto
Heifetz, Los Angeles Phil/
Wallenstein RCA LSB4015
Hoelscher, Süddeutscher Rundfunks/
Mattes EMI EMD5515

LALO, Edouard (1823–92)
Symphonie espagnole, Op. 21
Heifetz, RCA Symphony/Steinberg
RCA LSB4064
Kogan, Philharmonia/Kondrashin
Classics for Pleasure CFP40040
Menuhin, Philharmonia/Goossens
HMV ASD290*
Szeryng, Chicago Symphony/Hendl
RCA SB2120*

MARTIN, Frank (1890–1974)
Violin Concerto
Schneiderhan, Luxembourg Radio/
Martin Vox STGBY661

MARTINU, Bohuslav (1890–1959)
Violin Concerto No. 1 (1934)
Violin Concerto No. 2 (1943)
Suk, Czech Philharmonic/Neumann
Supraphon 1 10 1535

MENDELSSOHN, Felix (1809–47)
Concerto in E minor, Op. 64
Menuhin, Philharmonia/Süsskind
HMV ASD334
Grumiaux, Concertgebouw/Haitink
Philips 6580 022
Kreisler, LPO/Ronald (rec. 1928)
HMV HQM1104
Menuhin, LSO/Frühbeck de Burgos
HMV ASD2809
Szigeti, LPO/Beecham (rec. 1933)
HMV HLM7016
Milstein, Vienna Phil/Abbado
DG2530 359
Concerto in D minor, Op. posth.
Menuhin, LSO/Frühbeck de Burgos
HMV ASD2809

MILHAUD, Darius (1892–1974)
Violin Concerto No. 2 (1946)
Gertler, Prague Sym/Smetacek
Supraphon 110 1120
Violin Sonata No. 2 (1917)
Gertler, Andersen
Supraphon SUAST50483

MOZART, Wolfgang Amadeus
(1756–91)
*Violin Concertos (K207, 211, 216,
218, 219)*
*Concertone in C, K190, Sinfonia
concertante K364*
David and Igor Oistrakh/Berlin
Philharmonic HMV SLS828
Violin Concerto in B flat, K207
Szeryng, NPO/Gibson
Philips 6500 035
Grumiaux, LSO/Davis
Philips 6580 009

239

Violin and Viola

Violin Concerto No. 2 in D, K211
Grumiaux, LSO/Davis
        Philips SAL3492
Suk, Prague Chamber/Suk
        RCA LRL1 5084
Violin Concerto No. 3 in G, K216
Menuhin, Bath Festival Orchestra
        HMV ASD473
Szeryng, New Philharmonia/Gibson
        Philips 6500 036
Oistrakh, Berlin Philharmonic
        HMV ASD2988
Suk, Prague Chamber Orchestra
        RCA LRL1 5046
Loveday, Academy of St. Martin-in-
the-Fields/Marriner   Argo ZRG729
*Violin Concerto No. 4 in D major,
K218*
Grumiaux, LSO/Davis
        Philips 6580 009
Suk, Prague Chamber Orchestra
        RCA LRL1 5046
Menuhin, Bath Festival
        HMV ASD533*
*Violin Concerto No. 5 in A ('Turkish')
K219*
Michelucci, I Musici
        Philips 6500 537
Szeryng, NPO/Gibson
        Philips SAL3588
Oistrakh, Berlin Philharmonic
        HMV ASD2988
Menuhin, Bath Festival
        HMV ASD473
Violin Concerto No. 6 in E flat, K271a
Szeryng, NPO/Gibson
        Philips SAL3588
Menuhin, Bath Festival (cadenzas:
Enesco)   HMV ASD533*
*Sinfonia concertante in E flat, K364
(violin and viola)*
Grumiaux, Pelliccia, LSO/Davis
        Philips SAL3492
David and Igor Oistrakh, Moscow
PO/Kondrashin   Decca SXL6088
Stern, Zukerman, ECO/Barenboim
        CBS 73030
Concertone in C, K190
Hurwitz, Goren, ECO/Davis
        Oiseau Lyre SOL60030
Brown, Kaine, Academy of St.
Martins/Marriner
        Argo ZRG729
Serenade No. 7 in D major, K250
Staar, Vienna Mozart Ensemble/
Boskowsky   Decca SXL6614
Brandis, Berlin Philharmonic/Böhm
        DG2530 290
Maier, Collegium Aureum
        BASF BAC3015

Sonatas for violin and piano
C major, K296; E minor, K304;
A major, K526   Philips 6500 053
F major, K377; B flat, K378
        Philips 6500 054
B flat, K454; E flat, K481
        Philips 6500 055
D major, K306; E flat, K380;
Variations on *Hélas, j'ai perdu mon
amant*   Philips 6500 144
F major, K547; C major, K303;
E flat, K302; Variations on *La
Bergère Célimène*, K359
        Philips 6500 145
Henryk Szeryng, Ingrid Haebler

NIELSEN, Carl (1865–1931)
Violin Concerto, Op. 33
Menuhin, Danish Radio Orchestra/
Wöldike   HMV BLP1025*

PAGANINI, Niccolò (1782–1840)
Violin Concerto No. 1 in D, Op. 6
Perlman, RPO/Foster
        HMV ASD2782
Grumiaux, Monte Carlo Opera/
Bellugi   Philips 6500 411
Menuhin, RPO/Erede
        HMV ASD440
*Violin Concerto No. 2 in B minor,
Op. 7*
Ricci, LSO/Collins   Decca ECS654
Menuhin, RPO/Erede
        HMV ASD440
Violin Concerto No. 3 in E (1828)
Szeryng, LSO/Gibson
        Philips 6500 175
Violin Concerto No. 4 in D minor
Grumiaux, Monte Carlo Opera/
Bellugi   Philips 6500 411
*Violin Concerto No. 6 in E minor, Op.
Posth.*
Accardo, LPO/Dutoit   DG2530 467
Caprices, Op. 1
Perlman   HMV SLS832
Bradley   Classics for Pleasure
        CFP40062

PROKOFIEV, Serge (1891–1953)
Concerto No. 1 in D, Op. 19
Szigeti, LPO/Beecham (rec. 1935)
        HMV HLM7016
David Oistrakh, Moscow Radio/
Kondrashin   Saga 5160
Stern, Philadelphia Orchestra/
Ormandy   CBS 72269
Concerto No. 2 in G minor, Op. 63
Heifetz, Boston Symphony/Münch
        RCA LSB4048

David Oistrakh, Philharmonia/
Galliera   HMV SXLP30155
Stern, Philadelphia Orchestra/
Ormandy   CBS 72269
Szeryng, LSO/Rozhdestvesnky
                Philips SAL3571
Violin Sonata No. 1 in F minor, Op. 80
Oistrakh, Jampolsky
                HMV ALP1141
Perlman, Ashkenazy RCA LSB 4084
Violin Sonata No. 2 in D, Op. 94a
Perlman, Ashkenazy RCA LSB4084
Sonata for violin alone, Op. 115 (1947)
Jasek   Supraphon SUAST50707

RAVEL, Maurice (1875–1937)
Sonata for violin and piano (1920)
Voicou, Stefanescu Decca SDD352
Sonata for violin and cello (1922)
Kantorow, Rouvier
                Erato STU70789
Tzigane
Ricci, Suisse Romande/Ansermet
                Decca ECS670
Peinemann, Czech Philharmonic/
Maag   DG135147
Rosand, Süddeutscher Rundfunk/
Reinhardt   Turnabout TV34462S

SAINT-SAËNS, Camille (1835–1921)
*Violin Concerto No. 3 in B minor,
Op. 61*
Campoli, LSO/Gamba
                Decca ECS663
Milstein, Philharmonia/Fistoulari
                HMV SXLP30159
Szeryng, Monte Carlo Opera/
Remortel   Philips 6580 059
*Introduction and Rondo Capriccioso,
Op. 28*
Rosand, Südwestdeutscher
Rundfunk/Reichardt
                Turnabout TV34466S
Milstein, Philharmonia/Fistoulari
                HMV SXLP30159
Igor Oistrakh, Moscow Radio/
Rozhdestvesnky   HMV ASD2813
Havanaise, Op. 83
Rosand, Südwestdeutscher
Rundfunk/Reichardt
                Turnabout TV34462S

SARASATE, Pablo (1844–1908)
Carmen Fantasy Op. 25
Rosand, Südwestdeutscher
Rundfunk/Reichardt
                Turnabout TV34462S
Perlman, RPO/Foster
                HMV ASD2782

Zigeunerweisen, Op. 20, No. 1
Rosand, Südwestdeutscher
Rundfunk/Reichardt
                Turnabout TV34462S
Campoli, LSO/Gamba
                Decca ECS663

SCHOECK, Othmar (1886–1957)
Violin Concerto, Op. 21
Lehmann, The Zürcher Orchestra/
de Stoutz   MCS9047*

SCHOENBERG, Arnold
(1874–1951)
Violin Concerto, Op. 36 (1936)
Zeitlin, Bavarian Radio/Kubelik
                DG2530 257
Marschner, SWDR/Gielen
                Turnabout TV34051S

SCHUBERT, Franz (1797–1828)
Fantasia in C, D934
Pauk, Frankl   Vox STGBY611
Menuhin, Kentner HMV ASD475*
Sonata in A, D574
Kreisler, Rachmaninoff (rec. 1928)
                RCA VICS6059
Grumiaux, Veyron-Lacroix
                Philips 6500 341
*Sonatinas: D major, D384; A minor,
D385; G minor, D408*
Grumiaux, Veyron-Lacroix
                Philips 6500 341

SCHUMAN, William (b 1910)
Violin Concerto (1959)
Zukofsky, Boston Symphony/
Tilson Thomas   DG2530 103*

SCHUMANN, Robert (1810–56)
*Violin Concerto in D minor (1853
pub. 1937)*
Kulenkampff, Berlin Philharmonic/
Schmidt-Isserstedt
                Telefunken KT11008
*Violin Sonata No. 1 in A minor,
Op. 105*
Sivo, Buchbinder   Decca SDD401

SHOSTAKOVICH, Dmitri (1906-75)
Violin Concerto No. 1, Op. 99
David Oistrakh, NPO/Maxim
Shostakovich   HMV ASD2936
Violin Concerto No. 2, Op. 129
Oistrakh, Moscow Philharmonic/
Kondrashin   HMV ASD2447
Sonata, Op. 134
Oistrakh, Richter HMV ASD2718

SIBELIUS, Jean (1865–1957)
Violin Concerto in D minor, Op. 47
Kyung-Wha Chung, LSO/Previn
                Decca SXL6493

Violin and Viola

Ferras, Berlin Philharmonic/Karajan
DG138961
David Oistrakh, Moscow Radio/
Rozhdestvensky HMV ASD2407
Heifetz, Chicago Symphony/Hendl
RCA LSB4048
Heifetz, LPO/Beecham (rec. 1935)
World Records SH133
Szeryng, LSO/Rozhdestvensky
Philips SAL3571
Kulenkampff, Berlin Philharmonic/
Furtwängler Unicorn UN1107
Neveu, Philharmonia/Süsskind
HMV ALP1479*
Menuhin, LPO/Boult
HMV ALP1350*
Six Humoresques, Op. 87; Op. 89
Rosand, SWDR/Szoke
Turnabout TV34182S
Op. 87 only: Oistrakh, Moscow
Radio/Rozhdestvensky
HMV ASD2407

STRAVINSKY, Igor (1882–1971)
Violin Concerto in D (1931)
Stern, Columbia Symphony/
Stravinsky CBS S72038
David Oistrakh, Lamoureux
Orchestra/Haitink Philips 6580 003
Kyung-Wha Chung, LSO/Previn
Decca SXL6601
Duo concertante
Messiereur, Kozderkova
Supraphon SUAST50693

SUK, Josef (1874–1935)
Fantasy for violin and orchestra,
Op. 24 (1903)
Suk, Czech Philharmonic/Ancerl
Supraphon SUAST50777
Four Pieces, Op. 17
Suk, Panenka
Supraphon SUAST50777
Ginette and Jean Neveu
HMV ALP1479*

SZYMANOWSKI, Karol
(1882–1937)
Violin Concerto No. 1 (1917)
Oistrakh, Leningrad Philharmonic/
Sanderling Artia ALP156*
Violin Concerto No. 2, Op. 61 (1933)
Szeryng, Bamberg Symphony/Krenz
Philips 6500 421
Jasek, Prague Symphony/Turnovský
Supraphon SUAST50676

TARTINI, Giuseppe (1692–1770)
Violin Concertos
G major, D78; A major, D96; B flat
major, D117
Accardo, I Musici Philips 6500 784

TCHAIKOVSKY, Peter Ilyich
(1840–93)
Violin Concerto in D, Op. 35
Heifetz, Chicago Symphony/Reiner
RCA DPS2002
Elman, LPO/Boult Decca ECS569
Kogan, Paris Conservatoire/Silvestri
Classics for Pleasure CFP40083
Kyung-Wha Chung, LSO/Previn
Decca SXL6493
Igor Oistrakh, Moscow Phil/David
Oistrakh HMV ASD2813
Milstein, Vienna Philharmonic/
Abbado DG2530 359
Fujikawa, Rotterdam Sym/de Waart
Philips 6500 708
Serenade mélancolique, Op. 26
Kogan, Philharmonia/Kondrashin
Classics for Pleasure CFP40040
Grumiaux, NPO/de Waart
Philips 6580 047

TELEMANN, Georg Philipp
(1681–1767)
Concerto in F major for 3 violins and
strings (Tafelmusik Bk. II)
Academy of St. Martin-in-the-Fields/
Marriner Oiseau Lyre SOL264
Schola Cantorum Basiliensis/
Wenzinger DG135080
Viola Concerto in G
Academy of St. Martin-in-the-Fields/
Marriner Oiseau Lyre SOL276
Doktor, Concerto Amsterdam/
Brüggen Das Alte Werk SAWT9541
Concerto in G for two violas and
strings
Solisti di Zagreb/Janigro
HM17SD Vanguard

VAUGHAN WILLIAMS, Ralph
(1872–1958)
Concerto accademico in D minor
Buswell, LSO/Previn RCA SB6801
The Lark Ascending
Bean, NPO/Boult HMV ASD2329

VIEUXTEMPS, Henri (1820–81)
Concerto No. 5 in A minor, Op. 37
Zukerman, LSO/Mackerras
CBS S72828

VIOTTI, Giovanni (1755–1824)
Concerto No. 3 in A minor; No. 16 in
E minor; No. 24 in B minor
Rohn, ECO/Mackerras
DG2533 122
Concerto No. 22 in A minor
Lautenbacher, Berlin Sym/Bunte
Turnabout TV34229S

VIVALDI, Antonio (1678–1741)
Concertos, Op. 3 ('L'Estro Armonico')
Academy of St Martin-in-the-Fields/
Marriner   Argo ZRG733–4
Kuentz Chamber Orchestra
                          DG2726 001
Concertos, Op. 4 ('La Stravaganza')
Academy of St Martin-in-the-Fields/
Marriner   Argo ZRG800–01
*Concertos, Op. 8 ('Trial of Harmony
and Invention')*
Pierlot, Toso, Solisti Veneti/Scimone
                  Erato STU70679–81
Zukerman, ECO   CBS S78225
Concertos, Op. 9 ('La Cetra')
Ayo, Cotogni, I Musici
                     Philips 6703 012
*Concertos: E minor, P106; E major,
P246; Op. 12, No. 1*
Grumiaux, Dresden State Opera/
Negri   Philips 6500 690
*E minor, P106; D major, P208;
E major, P246; B flat, P419*
I Musici   Philips 6580 007

WALTON, William (b 1902)
Violin Concerto (1939)
Heifetz, Philharmonia/Walton
(rec. 1950)   RCA LSB4102
Menuhin, New Philharmonia/
Walton   HMV ASD2542

Francescatti, New York Phil/
Bernstein   CBS S61584
Kyung-Wha Chung, LSO/Previn
                     Decca SXL6601
Viola Concerto (1929 rev. 1961)
Menuhin, LSO/Walton
                     HMV ASD2542
Paul Doktor, LPO/Downes
                     CBS S61584

WIENIAWSKI, Henryk (1835–80)
*Violin Concerto No. 1 in F minor,
Op. 14*
Perlman, LPO/Ozawa
                     HMV ASD2870
*Violin Concerto No. 2 in D minor,
Op. 22*
Perlman, LPO/Ozawa
                     HMV ASD2870
Heifetz, RCA Symphony/Steinberg
                     RCA LSB4064
Szeryng, Bamberg Symphony/Krenz
                     Philips 6500 421
Legende, Op. 17
Campoli, LSO/Gamba
                     Decca ECS663
Grumiaux, NPO/de Waart
                     Philips 6580 047

WILLIAMSON, Malcolm (b 1931)
Violin Concerto (1965)
Menuhin, LPO/Boult
                     HMV ASD2759

Jealousy   EMD 5504
and
Fascinatin' Rhythm   EMD 5523
Yehudi Menuhin plays with
Stephane Grappelli

243

Index

Violin

Violin